Small Business Solutions

How to Fix and Prevent the Thirteen Biggest Problems That Derail Business

Robert Hisrich

McGraw-Hill

New York / Chicago / San Francisco / Lisbon
London / Madrid / Mexico City / Milan / New Delhi
San Juan / Singapore / Sydney / Toronto

The McGraw-Hill Companies

1 2 3 4 5 6 7 8 9 0 AGM/AGM 0 9 8 7 6 5 4 3

ISBN 0-07-141435-5

McGraw-Hill books are available at special discounts to use as premiums and sales promotions, or for use in corporate training programs. For more information, please write to the Director of Special Sales, Professional Publishing, McGraw-Hill, Two Penn Plaza, New York, NY 10121-2298. Or contact your local bookstore.

This book is printed on recycled, acid-free paper containing a minimum of 50% recycled de-inked paper.

Library of Congress Cataloging-in-Publication Data

Hisrich, Robert D.
Small business solutions : how to fix and prevent the 13 biggest problems that derail business / by Robert Hisrich.
p. cm.
ISBN 0-07-141435-5 (pbk. : alk. paper)
1. Small business—Management. 2. New business enterprises—Management. 3. Entrepreneurship. I. Title.
HD62.7.H577 2004
658.02'2—dc21

2003013496

To my wife Tina, my daughters Kary, Katy, and Kelly, and
my son-in-law Rich.
May you find entrepreneurial solutions to these 13 problems.

Contents

Preface

Starting and operating a new business involves considerable risk and effort to overcome the problems in creating and growing a new venture. These problems are so great that about 80–85% of all new ventures fail, are bought or folded into another company, or file for bankruptcy within the first five years of their existence. This book will help you as an entrepreneur or small business manager to avoid these outcomes and successfully manage and grow a business. By focusing on these 13 biggest problems, you can identify early on which of these problems are plaguing your business and adapt the solutions found in this book so that your business can continue to flourish.

This book is based on interviews with entrepreneurs and small business managers around the world. The discussion with these individuals centered around the question—what were your biggest problems and how did you fix them? Their responses, combined with my other research and experience in starting and growing several ventures, provided the basis for this book. The 13 problems are grouped into three areas—overall management, marketing, and finance. While there is no order to the importance of the problems, by recognizing the possibility of these problems (if they are not already occurring), benchmarks and early warning systems can be established and preventive measures enacted to help insure that these problems do not disrupt your business.

The first part—overall management—is appropriately the largest, as it deals with management issues and decisions involved in managing the small business. These seven problems in management are central to successfully launching, growing, and operating a small business. These managerially oriented problems include: not focusing (problem 1), not establishing the best organizational form (problem 2), not giving up control (problem 3), not attracting and retaining employees (problem 4), not choosing the right partner (problem 5), not being flexible and creative (problem 6), and not building a strong company (problem 7).

These managerially oriented problems are followed by three problems in marketing, which comprise the second part of the book. These problems are extremely important, as they affect a most important part of the business—obtaining sales and revenues. These three problems are: not focusing on a market niche and customers (problem 8); not doing international business (problem 9); and not growing your business (problem 10).

The final part of the book deals with an area that all small business managers and entrepreneurs can relate to—problems in finance. The first two of these problems are mentioned in most all articles discussing the lack of new venture creation and failure throughout the world—not raising enough capital (problem 11) and not managing the cash (problem 12). The book concludes with the thirteenth problem—not valuing the business.

Many people—entrepreneurs, small business managers, corporate executives, professors, and the publishing staff—have made this book possible. Of great assistance were the detailed comments of the editor and the assistance of the editorial team. My research assistants Nadia Tolshchikova and Sara Scarpetti provided research and editorial assistance, as did Teresa Kabat, who also helped prepare this manuscript in a timely manner.

I am deeply indebted to my wife Tina, my daughters Kary, Katy, and Kelly, and my son-in-law Rich for their understanding and support. It is to them and the generation they represent that this book is particularly dedicated.

Robert D. Hisrich

PART I

MANAGEMENT PROBLEMS

1

Staying Focused

PROFILE—JENNY MAXWELL AND LYNN DEREGOWSKI

When should pajamas be worn? Anytime, according to Jenny Maxwell and Lynn Deregowski, who in 1998 saw a need for chic and contemporary pajamas for people working or lounging at home. The two recognized a need for novelty pajamas while watching the popular television series *Will and Grace.* The characters wore stylish pajamas in most scenes. As a result, the two entrepreneurs started the Cat's Pajama Line. Their line of sleepwear, ranging from a backyard barbeque print to a cowgirl print to a sushi print to a Madison Avenue print, focuses on those individuals who want fashion not only in the bedroom but outside the bedroom as well. The two focused their business on a trend of people looking for something to escape everyday routine and make a statement, which has led to sales of over $1 million. It appears that novelty pajamas are a trend not only in the founders' state of California but also throughout the United States, which should bode well for sales in this and related lines in the foreseeable future.

Jenny Maxwell and Lynn Deregowski's story is one that frequently has less than a positive ending, as many entrepreneurs do not start with a good idea like the Cat's Pajama Line and then focus on this idea and successfully launch a business. This process is even more difficult owing to the numerous new products being regularly introduced. In 1991, over 32,000 new domestic products were introduced into the marketplace, almost twice the number introduced the year before. This increased volume of new products and the resulting hypercompetition creates problems for consumers, entrepreneurs, and inventors, in addition to the distribution system. Even when the distribution system decides to carry the new product, consumers can only buy so much. Obstacles in deciding on a good idea and then launching a new business based on this idea can indeed be overcome, as evidenced by the many entrepreneurs creating successful new ventures. This chapter addresses several of the issues in deciding on and focusing on a worthy idea: the entrepreneurial process; sources of new product and/or service ideas; evaluating the ideas and determining if the idea can be the basis of the business model; and focusing on operating the business and the business model created.

THE ENTREPRENEURIAL PROCESS

The sequence of activities in starting a new venture is embodied in the entrepreneurial process outlined in Table 1-1. Most entrepreneurs go through four phases in creating and operating a venture.

1. Identifying and evaluating an opportunity
2. Developing the business plan
3. Identifying the resources required to start the venture
4. Managing the new venture

Although the phases are progressive in nature, no phase is dealt with separately or is completed before proceeding to the next phase. For example, it is impossible to thoroughly analyze a potential opportunity without taking into account the resources required. By following the entrepreneurial process it will be easier to identify your idea and then focus your business on successfully developing and marketing this idea.

Table 1-1. Aspects of the entrepreneurial process.

Identify and Evaluate Opportunity	*Develop Business Plan*	*Identify Resources Required*	*Manage Enterprise*
• Creation and length of opportunity • Real and perceived value of opportunity • Risk and returns of opportunity • Competitive environment • Industry analysis • Opportunity versus personal skills and goals	• Title Page • Table of Contents • Executive Summary – Description of Business – Description of Industry – Technology Plan and Analysis – Marketing Plan – Financial Plan – Production Plan – Organization Plan – Operational Plan – Summary • Appendices (Exhibits)	• Existing resources of entrepreneur(s) • Resource gaps and available supplies • Access to needed resources	• Management style • Understand key variables for success • Identify problems and potential problems • Implement control systems • Develop growth strategy

IDENTIFYING THE OPPORTUNITY

Probably the most difficult task in the entrepreneurial process is identifying the right opportunity for the basis of the new venture. There are many opportunities that do not have the potential for developing a business model that makes sense for the market as well as for the entrepreneur. Since most good business opportunities do not magically appear, it is important for anyone interested in being an entrepreneur not only to be alert to *any* business possibility but also to establish procedures for identifying potential opportunities. One entrepreneur always asks at any cocktail or dinner event if anyone has an idea for a unique new product or service, no matter how crazy the idea may be. Another individual constantly monitors shopping patterns and behaviors in every store, periodically asking retail clerks about product problems or requests.

Sources of New Ideas

Some of the more frequently used sources of new ideas for entrepreneurs include consumers, existing companies, distribution channels, the federal government, and research and development.

Even with a wide variety of sources available, coming up with an idea to serve as the basis for a new venture can still be a difficult problem. The entrepreneur can use several methods to help generate and test new ideas, including focus groups, brainstorming, and problem inventory analysis.

Focus Groups

Focus groups have been used for a variety of purposes since the 1950s. A moderator leads a group of people through an open, in-depth discussion rather than simply asking questions to solicit participant response. For a new product area, the moderator focuses the discussion of the group in either a directive or a nondirective manner. The group of 8 to 14 participants is stimulated by comments from other group members in creatively conceptualizing and developing a new product idea to fulfill a market need. One company interested in the women's slipper market received its new product concept for a "warm and comfortable slipper that fits like an old shoe" from a focus group of 12 women from various socioeconomic backgrounds in the Boston area. The concept was developed into a new product that was a market success. The basis of the advertising message was formed by comments of other focus group members.

In addition to generating new ideas, the focus group is an excellent method for initially screening ideas and concepts. Using one of several procedures available, the results can be analyzed more quantitatively, making the focus group a useful method for both generating and evaluating product ideas.

Brainstorming

The brainstorming method for generating new product ideas is based on the fact that people can be stimulated to greater creativity by meeting with others and participating in organized group experiences. Although most of the ideas generated from the group have no basis for further development, sometimes a good idea emerges. This has a greater frequency of occurrence when the brainstorming effort focuses on a specific product or market area.

A large commercial bank successfully used brainstorming to develop a journal that would provide quality information to their industrial clients. The brainstorming among executives focused on the characteristics of the market, the information content, the frequency of issue, and the promotional value of the journal to the bank. Once the general format and issue frequency were determined, focus groups of vice presidents of finance of Fortune 1000 companies were undertaken in three cities—Boston, Chicago, and Dallas—to discuss the new journal content and its relevancy and value to them.

Problem Inventory Analysis

Problem inventory analysis uses individuals in a manner that is analogous to focus groups to generate new product ideas. However, instead of generating new ideas themselves, consumers are provided with a list of problems in a general product category. They are then asked to identify and discuss products in this category that have the particular problem. This method is effective since it is easier to relate known products to suggested problems and arrive at a new product idea than to generate an entirely new product idea by itself. Problem inventory analysis can also be used to test a new product idea.

Results from problem inventory analysis must be carefully evaluated because they may not be the basis for a business model and therefore do not actually reflect a new business opportunity. For example, General Foods' introduction of a compact cereal box in response to the problem that the available boxes did not fit well on the shelf was not successful. The perceived problem of package size had little effect on actual purchasing behavior. To ensure the best results, problem inventory analysis should be used primarily to identify product ideas for further evaluation.

Evaluating the Opportunity

Whether the opportunity is identified by using input from consumers, business associates, channel members, or technical people, each opportunity must be carefully screened and evaluated. This evaluation of the opportunity is perhaps the most critical element of the entrepreneurial process as it allows the entrepreneur to assess whether the specific product or service has the returns needed for the resources required. As indicated in Table 1-2, this evaluation process involves looking at the creation and length of the opportunity, its real and perceived value(s), its risks and returns, its competitive environment, its industry, and its fit with the personal skills and goals of the entrepreneur.

It is important for the entrepreneur to understand the cause of the opportunity. Is it technological change, market shift, government regulation, or competition? These factors and the resulting opportunity have a different market size and time dimension.

The market size and the length of the window of opportunity form the primary basis for determining the risks and rewards

Table 1-2. Determining the need for a new product idea.

Factor	Aspects	Competitive Capabilities	New Product Ideas Capability
Type of need Continuing need Declining need Emerging need Future need			
Timing of need Duration of need Frequency of need Demand cycle Position in life cycle			
Competing ways to satisfy need Doing without Using present way Modifying present way			
Perceived benefits/risks Utility to customer Appeal characteristics Customer tastes and preferences Buying motives Consumption habits			
Price versus performance features Price-quantity relationship Demand elasticity Stability of price Stability of market			
Market size and potential Market growth Market trends Market development requirements Threats to market			
Availability to customer funds General economic conditions Economic trends Customer income Financing opportunities			

Source: Reprinted with permission of Macmillan College Publishing Company, from *Marketing Decisions for New and Mature Products*, 2nd/ed., by Robert D. Hisrich and Michael P. Peters, ©1991 by Macmillan College Publishing Company, Inc., p. 190.

involved. The risks reflect the market, competition, technology, and amount of capital involved. The amount of capital forms the basis for the return and rewards.

In this evaluation, the competition and potential competition also must be carefully appraised. Features and potential price for the idea should be evaluated along with those of competitive products presently in the product/market space. If any major problems and competitive disadvantages are identified early on, modifications to the idea can be made or the idea dropped and new ones investigated.

The relative advantages of the new idea versus competitive products can be determined through the following questions. How does the new idea compare with competitive products in terms of quality and reliability? Is the idea superior or deficient compared with products currently available in the market? Is this a good market opportunity?

One method for evaluating the idea against competing products or services is the conversational interview. Here, selected individuals are asked to compare the idea against products presently filling that need. By comparing the characteristics and attributes of the new idea, some uniqueness of the idea can be forthcoming.

An initial industry analysis should determine if there is really a need for as well as the value of the idea. In order to accurately determine the need, it is helpful to define the potential needs of the market in terms of timing, satisfaction, alternatives, benefits and risks, future expectations, price-versus-product performance features, market structure and size, and economic conditions. A form for helping in this need determination is shown in Table 1-2. The factors indicated in this table should be evaluated not only in terms of the characteristics of the idea but also in terms of the idea's competitive strength relative to each factor. This comparison with competitive products will indicate the strengths and weaknesses of the idea.

The need determination should focus on the type of need, its timing, the users involved with trying it, the importance of controllable marketing variables, the overall market structure, and the characteristics of the market. Each of these factors should be evaluated in terms of characteristics of the new idea being considered and the aspects and capabilities of present methods for satisfying the particular need. This analysis will indicate the extent of the opportunity available.

In determining the value of the idea, financial scheduling—such as cash outflow, cash inflow, contribution to profit, and return on investment—needs to be evaluated in terms of other ideas. Using the form indicated in Table 1-3, the dollar amount of each of the considerations important to the new idea should be determined as accurately as possible so that a quantitative evaluation can be made. These figures can then be revised as better information becomes available.

Finally, the opportunity also must fit the personal skills and goals of the entrepreneur. It is particularly important that the entrepreneur be able to put forth the necessary time and effort required to make the venture succeed. Although many entrepreneurs feel that the desire can be developed along with the venture, typically it does not materialize, therefore dooming the venture to failure. An entrepreneur must believe in the idea so much that he or she will make the necessary sacrifices to develop the idea into a sound business model that is the basis for a successful new venture. This should lead to developing an opportunity assessment plan.

Opportunity Assessment Plan

Opportunity analysis, or what is frequently called an opportunity assessment plan, is not a business plan. Compared to a business plan, it should be shorter; it should focus on the opportunity, not the entire venture; and it should provide the basis for making the decision of whether or not to act on the opportunity.

An opportunity analysis plan includes the following: a description of the product or service, an assessment of the opportunity, an assessment of the entrepreneur and the team, specifications of all the activities and resources needed to translate the opportunity into a viable business model and venture, and the source of capital to

Table 1-3. Determining the value of a new product idea.

Value Consideration	Cost (in $)
Cash outflow	
R&D costs	
Marketing costs	
Capital equipment costs	
Other costs	
Cash inflow	
Sales of new product	
Effect on additional sales	
Salvageable value	
Net cash flow	
Maximum exposure	
Time to maximum exposure	
Duration of exposure	
Total investment	
Maximum net cash in a single year	
Profit	
Profit from new product	
Profit affecting additional sales of existing products	
Fraction of total company profit	
Relative return	
Return on shareholder's equity (ROE)	
Return on investment (ROI)	
Cost of capital	
Present value (PV)	
Discounted cash flow (DCF)	
Return on assets employed (ROA)	
Return on sales	
Compared to other investments	
Compared to other product opportunities	
Compared to other investment opportunities	

Source: Reprinted with permission of Macmillan College Publishing Company, from *Marketing Decisions for New and Mature Products*, 2nd ed., by Robert D. Hisrich and Michael P. Peters, ©1991 by Macmillan College Publishing Company, Inc., p. 196.

finance the initial venture as well as its growth—first- and second-stage financing. The most difficult and critical aspect of opportunity analysis is the assessment of the opportunity. This requires answering the following questions:

- What market need does it fill?
- What personal observations have you experienced or recorded with regard to that market need?
- What social conditions underlie this market need?
- What market research data can be obtained to describe this market need?
- What patents might be available to fulfill this need?
- What competition exists in this market? How would you describe the behavior of this competition?
- What does the international market look like?
- What does the international competition look like?
- Where is the money to be made in this activity?

Develop a Business Plan

Following identifying and evaluating the opportunity, the second phase in the entrepreneurial process is developing a good business plan to exploit the defined opportunity. This is perhaps the most time-consuming and difficult phase of the entrepreneurial process. An entrepreneur often has not prepared a business plan before and does not have the time or resources available. A good business plan is not only important in developing the opportunity but also essential in determining the resources required, obtaining those resources, and successfully managing the resulting venture.

Resources Needed

The third phase of the entrepreneurial process (see Table 1-1) is determining the resources needed for exploiting the opportunity and developing a new venture. This process starts with an appraisal of the entrepreneur's present resources. Any resources that are critical must then be distinguished from those that are just helpful. Care must be taken not to underestimate the amount and variety of resources needed. The downside risks associated with insufficient or inappropriate resources also should be assessed.

Acquiring the needed resources in a timely manner while giving up as little control as possible is a difficult step in the entrepreneurial process. An entrepreneur should strive to maintain as large a position of ownership as possible, particularly in the start-up stage. As the business develops, more funds will probably be needed to finance the growth of the venture, requiring more ownership to be relinquished. Alternative suppliers of these resources, along with their needs and desires, need to be identified. By understanding resource supplier needs, the entrepreneur can structure a deal that enables the resources to be acquired at the lowest possible cost and with the least loss of control.

Manage the Enterprise

After resources have been acquired, the entrepreneur must employ them through the implementation of the business plan. Managing the enterprise is the last phase of the entrepreneurial process and includes examining the operational problems of the growing enterprise. This involves implementing a management style and structure, as well as determining the key variables for success. A control system must be established so that any problem areas are carefully monitored and identified. Some entrepreneurs have difficulty managing and growing the venture they created. This is one difference between entrepreneurial and managerial decision making.

CREATING THE BUSINESS MODEL AND BUSINESS

Once the opportunity passes all the evaluation criteria, it is important to see if it can be the basis for a business model. A business model is the entire picture of how a company does business including all its strategies and tactics. This business model should be compared to all other business models operating in the product/market space to determine the uniqueness. Usually this uniqueness comes from one of three sources. The first source, which is not company specific, comes from a new "technology" often introduced from another industry. Companies making coffee such as Folgers and Maxwell House were continuously monitoring each other but were blindsided when Starbucks, a retail coffee house, started selling coffee along with its already brewed products. The second source is from customers, such as when the existing customer base changes dramatically or when new customers want something similar, but enhanced. Pizza Hut changed the business model of pizza sales by introducing the home delivery of pizzas. Mazzios changed the business model again by having the customer's previous transaction appear from a database onto the order-taking screen, providing the customer more personalized treatment as well as the opportunity for cross-selling.

The final source of change comes from capital allocation or pricing. Often established firms are not interested in developing a new business model that might lose money or require hard data when it is not possible to obtain. Michael Dell changed the business model in the computer industry by building computers to order and selling them via the Internet.

The business model developed should have about three to five aspects that make it unique and differentiate it from any business model on the market. These unique aspects, often referred to as the unique selling proposition, form the basis for the direction and promotion of the company.

FOCUS, FOCUS, FOCUS

Once the business model has been operationalized and the new venture is operating and growing, it is important to use the business model to shape and manage the future direction of the venture. This ability to define a business model and then focus on operating it, instead of always changing and coming up with new ideas and solutions, is one differentiating aspect of an entrepreneur and an inventor.

An *inventor,* an individual who creates something for the first time, is a highly driven individual motivated by his or her own work and personal ideas. A typical inventor places a high premium on being an achiever and measures achievement by the number of inventions developed and the number of patents granted.

As indicated in this profile, an inventor differs considerably from an entrepreneur. An *entrepreneur* is someone who creates something new with value by devoting the necessary time and effort, assuming the accompanying financial, psychic, and social risks, and receiving the resulting rewards of monetary and personal satisfaction and independence. Whereas an entrepreneur falls in love with the organization (the new venture) and will do almost anything to ensure its growth and survival, an inventor falls in love with the invention and will only reluctantly modify the invention to make it more commercially feasible. The development of a new venture based on an inventor's work often requires the expertise of an entrepreneur and a team approach to new venture creation.

An entrepreneur and the management team need to make sure they are not distracted by other inventions and opportunities and must focus, focus, focus on carrying out the business model developed. A lack of focus is one of the most often cited reasons by capital providers, such as venture capitalists, for problems in developing and growing a venture and one of the main causes of business failure.

2

Establishing the Best Organizational Form

PROFILE—WILSON ALERS

Wilson Alers, founder and president of Media Stage Inc., knows the importance of a good advisor. In 1990, he started the company with two partners to service business events such as stockholders' and other corporate meetings. The company established its checking account at Bank of America, in part because Wilson had his personal banking account at a predecessor bank—NCNB. As Media Stage grew, so did the company's use of the bank's services—from financing the purchase of equipment to financing the construction of the company's headquarters. In this construction financing, Bank of America was particularly helpful as it worked with the Small Business Administration to develop a loan requiring only 10 percent cash equity instead of the typical 20 percent.

Media Stage Inc., under Wilson Alers's direction, has continued to grow into a corporate presentation and audiovisual service company and now has 22 full-time employees and 18 additional technicians during busy sales months. The banking relationship also has evolved with the addition of Steven Merrell, a small business senior client manager, being one of the company's business advisors. Steven Merrell recently helped the company secure a line of credit and finance a loan with Bank of America. And who do you think was the first person called when Wilson Alers was concerned about the impact of the terrorist attacks of September 11, 2001, on his overall business and financial situation? Steven Merrell, of course.

Although this was not the case with Media Stage Inc. and Wilson Alers, one of the biggest mistakes entrepreneurs can make is not seeking the right individuals for advice as well as not establishing the right organizational form and structure. This chapter focuses on these issues, including using a board of directors and a board of advisors, and concludes with some suggestions for maximizing the effectiveness of any advisory group.

ORGANIZATIONAL FORM

Choosing the right organizational form has far-reaching consequences for the growth and future success of the business model developed. The decision is complex, with some technicalities involved, and is made more difficult by the changes in the laws and the rules and regulations affecting various organizational forms.

When choosing the right organizational form for your business, several factors need to be considered: (1) risk, in terms of liability; (2) finance, in terms of raising capital and tax considerations; (3) control, in terms of who controls the business; (4) equity, in terms of who owns the equity; and (5) continuity, in terms of transferring ownership. In light of these factors, an entrepreneur can choose several different organizational forms: sole proprietorship, general partnership, limited partnership, limited liability company (LLC), or a corporation. And there are several types of corporations. Each of these organizations will be discussed in turn.

Sole Proprietorship

A sole proprietorship is a so-called one-man band. This organizational form has no organizational formalities and no name requirement. The entrepreneur has full management authority accompanied by full personal liability for any and all business obligations. The earnings of a sole proprietorship are taxed on the basis of the personal income tax return of the entrepreneur. The sole proprietorship has the same business life as the life of the owner.

General and Limited Partnerships

A general partnership involves two or more individuals who have a partnership agreement to operate a business and share the earnings and liabilities of the venture. While the partnership agreement may be oral, it is highly recommended that a written agreement be drafted using legal council so that each individual involved understands all aspects of the agreement. This written agreement becomes particularly important when significant financial gains or losses occur or when liability issues arise. To set up a general partnership company, the entrepreneur does not have to file with the state of the company's domicile unless he or she wants to use a trade or fictitious name. The profits and losses are allocated based on capital contribution of each individual or the terms of the partnership agreement. The profits and losses realized are passed through and reflected on each individual's personal income tax return. Each partner is liable for all business obligations, making the business liability aspect of a general partnership a significant concern.

While a limited partnership also has two or more owners, it differs from a general partnership in that there are two classes of partners: general partners, who have no limited liability, and limited partners, who have limited liability. The general partner(s) handles the day-to-day operations of the business, making all the decisions, while the limited partners are passive investors with no involvement in the daily operations of the business. This organizational form is a common one in real estate investments and venture capital companies. To establish this form of organization, the entrepreneur must file with the secretary of the state where the company is domiciled. The sharing of the profits and losses of a limited partnership are based on the capital contributions or the terms of the agreement, with these being passed through and reflected on each partner's personal income tax return.

The general partners are liable for all business obligations and have fiduciary responsibility to each other. As long as the limited partner's name is not in the partnership name and the limited partner does not participate in the management of the partnership, he or she has no personal liability for the business obligations of the partnership.

Limited Liability Company

The limited liability company (LLC) is a relatively new form of business organization. State laws vary significantly on LLCs, so the choice of state of filing is most important in this organizational form. Some states, such as Alaska, Delaware, and Nevada, have more favorable liability laws for LLCs than do other states. The LLC has a board of directors and officers, with the management being done by members of the board or by designated managers. The interests in an LLC are called *units*. An LLC can be taxed as a partnership, with taxes passed through to the member units, or as a corporation. Since the membership units are securities, LLCs need to comply with state and federal securities laws. Memberships can be transferred according to the terms in the operating agreement.

Corporation

The corporation is the most well known form of business organization. A corporation is a distinct legal entity, a function of state law, which files its own tax return. Corporations have several distinct characteristics: limited liability, centralized management, transferability of shares, and continuity of existence. Probably the most important characteristic of a corporation is that it provides limited liability by being a separate legal entity that may own property, have employees, incur liabilities, make contracts, and pay taxes. The risk to the shareholders is limited to the capital invested unless the corporation is not carefully separated from the individuals. An entrepreneur needs to make sure that he or she is separately identified from the corporation and that separate bank accounts are maintained for the corporation and the entrepreneur. If this practice is not in place, the entrepreneur also can be held liable.

Another characteristic of a corporation is centralized management, which reports and is subject to the shareholders. The corporation is managed under the direction of a board of directors.

Ownership in a corporation is represented by shares of stock, which can be transferred to others. Shareholders can restrict transfer of stock initially by having in the corporation by-laws the right of first refusal. This by-law dictates how shares must first be offered for sale before selling to others.

The final characteristic of a corporation is its continuity. Unless limited by the articles of incorporation, a corporation's life is perpetual.

There are several types of corporations including: (1) regular C corporations, (2) S corporations, (3) professional corporations, (4) close corporations, and (5) nonprofit corporations.

Regular C Corporation

A regular C corporation has been an organizational form for a long period of time and is a separate legal entity having a very flexible capital structure—it can issue various classes of stock with varied distribution and voting rights. While the advantages of a regular C corporation are many, there are three disadvantages: double taxation, trapping of losses, and separate state franchise tax. A regular C corporation pays corporate income tax on its profits, and its shareholders are taxed on any dividends issued at their ordinary income tax rates, therefore causing a double taxation. Second, the losses of a regular C corporation are carried forward, not realized right away, and are used to offset income in the future. Finally, a regular C corporation is subject to a separate state franchise tax, which does not occur with other types of corporations.

Subchapter S Corporation

The second type of corporation—a subchapter S corporation—is a more recent form of corporation that is its own legal entity and has the same liability as a regular C corporation. The main advantage of a subchapter S corporation is that it avoids double taxation as all profits of the corporation are passed through as dividends to the shareholders. In this way the individual shareholders are the only ones taxed, just like in a partnership. All shareholders must agree to this either initially or when a regular C corporation is changed to an S corporation. In an S corporation there can be no more than 75 individual shareholders. While there is only one class of stock, there can be voting and nonvoting common stock. No preferred stock can be issued.

Professional Corporation

The remaining three types of corporation are not as widely used as C or S corporations. The professional corporation is a way for professionals, such as doctors, dentists, lawyers, and licensed professionals like engineering consultants, to incorporate. The type of professionals that can use this organizational form is limited. While an engineering consulting firm can establish a professional corporation, a management consulting firm cannot. While the professional corporation is the legal entity for tax and liability purposes, this does not absolve the professional for personal liability if negligent practice occurs.

Close Corporation

Another lesser-used corporation—the close corporation—requires that all shareholders sign the close corporation agreement. This form of organization provides significant flexibility because a close corporation can operate as a partnership with no board of directors and no annual meetings.

Nonprofit Corporation

The final type of corporation is the nonprofit corporation. This allows individuals to form an organization for charitable or other specific purposes such as a trade organization or a union. The corporation itself is tax exempt and contributions are deductible as well. While a nonprofit corporation can make a profit, all profits must be reinvested for the purpose of the organization.

FILING AND ESTABLISHING THE ORGANIZATION

Since the formation of an organization is a function of state law, an entrepreneur must file for one of the previously discussed organizational forms in the state where he or she wants to locate the business. While many companies used to file their organization papers in Delaware due to their pro-business laws even though they located their headquarters in another state, this practice has decreased in the last several years. Today, most states have the same laws as Delaware, so there is no significant advantage in establishing your firm in a state other than the one where you live.

The process of establishing a regular C corporation is quite straightforward. You first want to check the name availability for your company, including such titles as "Company," "Co.," "Corporation," "Corp.," or "Inc." You then want to file your articles of incorporation with the secretary of state. The process is not very difficult and can be done in a very short period of time. In Ohio, as in most other states, the filing can be done on the Internet using a credit card to cover the filing fee—around $125. Once the articles of incorporation are filed, you must then apply to the Internal Revenue Service (IRS) for an employer ID number using Form SS-4, shown in Figure 2-1. You need to have an employer ID number in the United States in order to operate a business and do such things as open a bank account. Finally, you must apply to the appropriate state agencies where your company is located for workers' compensation, sales tax, unemployment, and any other needed licenses or permits.

Forming an LLC follows the same procedures as those of a corporation except that the forms for filing the articles of organization are different from the initial articles of incorporation. Also, there is an additional form required, depending on whether it is a single-member LLC or a multimember LLC. The same is true for a limited partnership, except a certificate of limited partnership and the limited partnership agreement also must be filed.

Form **SS-4**
(Rev. December 2001)
Department of the Treasury
Internal Revenue Service

Application for Employer Identification Number
(For use by employers, corporations, partnerships, trusts, estates, churches, government agencies, Indian tribal entities, certain individuals, and others.)
► **See separate instructions for each line.** ► **Keep a copy for your records.**

EIN
OMB No. 1545-0003

Type or print clearly.

1 Legal name of entity (or individual) for whom the EIN is being requested

2 Trade name of business (if different from name on line 1) | 3 Executor, trustee, "care of" name

4a Mailing address (room, apt., suite no. and street, or P.O. box) | 5a Street address (if different) (Do not enter a P.O. box.)

4b City, state, and ZIP code | 5b City, state, and ZIP code

6 County and state where principal business is located

7a Name of principal officer, general partner, grantor, owner, or trustor | 7b SSN, ITIN, or EIN

8a **Type of entity** (check only one box)
☐ Sole proprietor (SSN)
☐ Partnership
☐ Corporation (enter form number to be filed) ►
☐ Personal service corp.
☐ Church or church-controlled organization
☐ Other nonprofit organization (specify) ►
☐ Other (specify) ►
☐ Estate (SSN of decedent)
☐ Plan administrator (SSN)
☐ Trust (SSN of grantor)
☐ National Guard ☐ State/local government
☐ Farmers' cooperative ☐ Federal government/military
☐ REMIC ☐ Indian tribal governments/enterprises
Group Exemption Number (GEN) ►

8b If a corporation, name the state or foreign country (if applicable) where incorporated | State | Foreign country

9 **Reason for applying** (check only one box)
☐ Started new business (specify type) ►
☐ Hired employees (Check the box and see line 12.)
☐ Compliance with IRS withholding regulations
☐ Other (specify) ►
☐ Banking purpose (specify purpose) ►
☐ Changed type of organization (specify new type) ►
☐ Purchased going business
☐ Created a trust (specify type) ►
☐ Created a pension plan (specify type) ►

10 Date business started or acquired (month, day, year) | 11 Closing month of accounting year

12 First date wages or annuities were paid or will be paid (month, day, year). **Note:** *If applicant is a withholding agent, enter date income will first be paid to nonresident alien. (month, day, year)* . . . . ►

13 Highest number of employees expected in the next 12 months. **Note:** *If the applicant does not expect to have any employees during the period, enter "-0-."* . . . . ► | Agricultural | Household | Other

14 Check **one** box that best describes the principal activity of your business.
☐ Health care & social assistance ☐ Wholesale-agent/broker
☐ Construction ☐ Rental & leasing ☐ Transportation & warehousing ☐ Accommodation & food service ☐ Wholesale-other ☐ Retail
☐ Real estate ☐ Manufacturing ☐ Finance & insurance ☐ Other (specify)

15 Indicate principal line of merchandise sold; specific construction work done; products produced; or services provided.

16a Has the applicant ever applied for an employer identification number for this or any other business? . . . . ☐ **Yes** ☐ **No**
Note: *If "Yes," please complete lines 16b and 16c.*

16b If you checked "Yes" on line 16a, give applicant's legal name and trade name shown on prior application if different from line 1 or 2 above.
Legal name ► Trade name ►

16c Approximate date when, and city and state where, the application was filed. Enter previous employer identification number if known.
Approximate date when filed (mo., day, year) | City and state where filed | Previous EIN

Third Party Designee
Complete this section **only** if you want to authorize the named individual to receive the entity's EIN and answer questions about the completion of this form.
Designee's name | Designee's telephone number (include area code) ( )
Address and ZIP code | Designee's fax number (include area code) ( )

Under penalties of perjury, I declare that I have examined this application, and to the best of my knowledge and belief, it is true, correct, and complete.
Applicant's telephone number (include area code) ( )
Name and title (type or print clearly) ►
Applicant's fax number (include area code) ( )
Signature ► Date ►

For Privacy Act and Paperwork Reduction Act Notice, see separate instructions. Cat. No. 16055N Form **SS-4** (Rev. 12-2001)

Figure 2–1. Form SS-4, application for employer identification number.

Do I Need an EIN?

File Form SS-4 if the applicant entity does not already have an EIN but is required to show an EIN on any return, statement, or other document.[1] **See also the separate instructions for each line on Form SS-4.**

IF the applicant...	AND...	THEN...
Started a new business	Does not currently have (nor expect to have) employees	Complete lines 1, 2, 4a-6, 8a, and 9-16c.
Hired (or will hire) employees, including household employees	Does not already have an EIN	Complete lines 1, 2, 4a-6, 7a-b (if applicable), 8a, 8b (if applicable), and 9-16c.
Opened a bank account	Needs an EIN for banking purposes only	Complete lines 1-5b, 7a-b (if applicable), 8a, 9, and 16a-c.
Changed type of organization	Either the legal character of the organization or its ownership changed (e.g., you incorporate a sole proprietorship or form a partnership)[2]	Complete lines 1-16c (as applicable).
Purchased a going business[3]	Does not already have an EIN	Complete lines 1-16c (as applicable).
Created a trust	The trust is other than a grantor trust or an IRA trust[4]	Complete lines 1-16c (as applicable).
Created a pension plan as a plan administrator[5]	Needs an EIN for reporting purposes	Complete lines 1, 2, 4a-6, 8a, 9, and 16a-c.
Is a foreign person needing an EIN to comply with IRS withholding regulations	Needs an EIN to complete a Form W-8 (other than Form W-8ECI), avoid withholding on portfolio assets, or claim tax treaty benefits[6]	Complete lines 1-5b, 7a-b (SSN or ITIN optional), 8a-9, and 16a-c.
Is administering an estate	Needs an EIN to report estate income on Form 1041	Complete lines 1, 3, 4a-b, 8a, 9, and 16a-c.
Is a withholding agent for taxes on non-wage income paid to an alien (i.e., individual, corporation, or partnership, etc.)	Is an agent, broker, fiduciary, manager, tenant, or spouse who is required to file **Form 1042,** Annual Withholding Tax Return for U.S. Source Income of Foreign Persons	Complete lines 1, 2, 3 (if applicable), 4a-5b, 7a-b (if applicable), 8a, 9, and 16a-c.
Is a state or local agency	Serves as a tax reporting agent for public assistance recipients under Rev. Proc. 80-4, 1980-1 C.B. 581[7]	Complete lines 1, 2, 4a-5b, 8a, 9, and 16a-c.
Is a single-member LLC	Needs an EIN to file **Form 8832,** Classification Election, for filing employment tax returns, **or** for state reporting purposes[8]	Complete lines 1-16c (as applicable).
Is an S corporation	Needs an EIN to file **Form 2553,** Election by a Small Business Corporation[9]	Complete lines 1-16c (as applicable).

[1] For example, a sole proprietorship or self-employed farmer who establishes a qualified retirement plan, or is required to file excise, employment, alcohol, tobacco, or firearms returns, must have an EIN. **A partnership, corporation, REMIC (real estate mortgage investment conduit), nonprofit organization (church, club, etc.), or farmers' cooperative must use an EIN for any tax-related purpose even if the entity does not have employees.**

[2] However, **do not** apply for a new EIN if the existing entity only **(a)** changed its business name, **(b)** elected on Form 8832 to change the way it is taxed (or is covered by the default rules), or **(c)** terminated its partnership status because at least 50% of the total interests in partnership capital and profits were sold or exchanged within a 12-month period. (The EIN of the terminated partnership should continue to be used. See Regulations section 301.6109-1(d)(2)(iii).)

[3] Do not use the EIN of the prior business unless you became the "owner" of a corporation by acquiring its stock.

[4] However, IRA trusts that are required to file **Form 990-T,** Exempt Organization Business Income Tax Return, must have an EIN.

[5] A plan administrator is the person or group of persons specified as the administrator by the instrument under which the plan is operated.

[6] Entities applying to be a Qualified Intermediary (QI) need a QI-EIN even if they already have an EIN. **See Rev. Proc. 2000-12.**

[7] See also *Household employer* on page 4. (**Note:** State or local agencies may need an EIN for other reasons, e.g., hired employees.)

[8] Most LLCs **do not** need to file Form 8832. See **Limited liability company (LLC)** on page 4 for details on completing Form SS-4 for an LLC.

[9] An existing corporation that is electing or revoking S corporation status should use its previously-assigned EIN.

Figure 2–1. (*Continued*)

ESTABLISHING THE BEST ORGANIZATIONAL DESIGN

Usually, the design of the initial organization will be simple. In fact, the entrepreneur may find that he or she performs all the functions of the organization. This is a common problem and cause for many failures, as the entrepreneur sometimes thinks he or she can do everything and is unwilling to give up the responsibility to others or even to include others. As the workload increases, the organizational structure will need to expand to include additional employees with defined roles within the organization. Effective interviewing and hiring procedures will need to be implemented to ensure that these new employees will assimilate effectively into the new venture.

For many new ventures, predominantly part-time employees are hired, raising important issues of commitment and loyalty. Regardless of the number of actual personnel involved in running the venture, the organization must identify the major activities required to operate it effectively and assign individuals to accomplish these activities.

The design of the organization, indicated in the organizational chart, shows the relationships within and responsibilities of the organization. Typically these can be grouped into the following areas:

- *Organization Structure*. This defines the jobs of each function and individual and the communication and relationship these jobs have with each other. These relationships are depicted in an organization chart.
- *Planning, Measurement, and Evaluation Schemes*. All organization activities should reflect the goals and objectives underlying the venture's existence. The entrepreneur must spell out how these goals will be achieved (plans) and how they will be measured and evaluated.
- *Rewards*. Members of an organization require rewards in the form of promotions, bonuses, and praise. The entrepreneur or other key managers are responsible for these rewards.
- *Selection Criteria*. The entrepreneur will need to determine a set of guidelines for selecting individuals for each position.
- *Training*. Training, on or off the job, needs to occur, particularly as the organization grows. This training may be in the form of formal education or practical learning skills.

Organizational Design

The organization's design can be very simple or more complex. Figure 2-2 illustrates an early stage of development in an organization. Here, the new venture is operated by a few people, possibly even only one—the entrepreneur. This organizational chart reflects the activities of the firm in production, marketing/sales, and administration. Initially, the entrepreneur may manage all these functions. At this stage, there is no need for submanagers; the entrepreneur deals with everyone involved in the business and all aspects of the operation.

As the business expands, the organization may be more appropriately described by a more advanced organizational design. Here submanagers are hired to coordinate, organize, and control various aspects of the business. The production manager is responsible for quality control and assembly of the finished product by the subcontractor. The marketing manager develops promotion and advertising strategy and coordinates the efforts of the expanding rep organization.

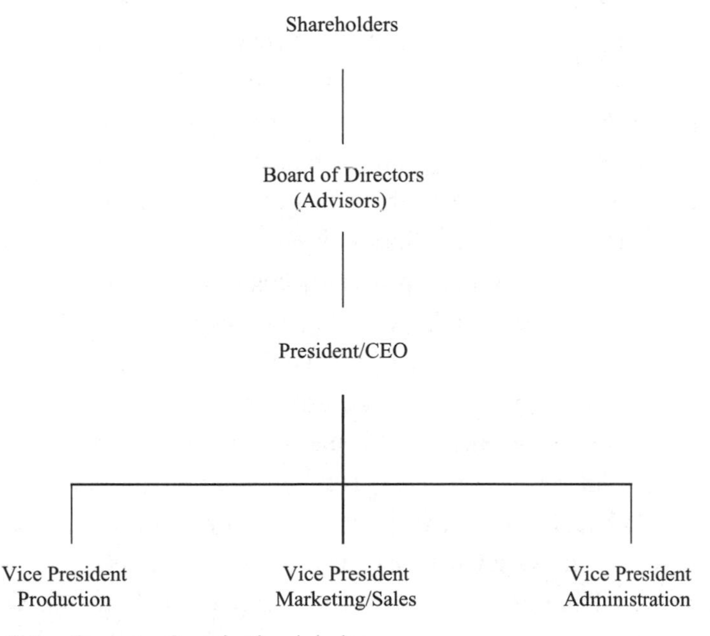

Figure 2-2. Stage 1—Organizational design.

The administrative manager assumes the responsibility for all administrative tasks in the business operation. Now the elements of measurement, evaluation, rewards, selection, and training become important.

As the organization evolves, the entrepreneur's decision roles also need to change to remain effective. The entrepreneur also will need to respond to pressures such as an unsatisfied customer, a supplier not fulfilling a contract, or a key employee threatening to quit. Much of the entrepreneur's time in the start-up will be spent "putting out fires."

Another role for the entrepreneur is obtaining and allocating resources. This involves designing the budgets and assigning the responsibilities for using the funds allocated. The allocation of resources can be a very complex and difficult process for the entrepreneur since one decision can significantly affect another. The final decision role of the entrepreneur is that of negotiator. Negotiations of contracts, salaries, and prices of raw materials are an integral part of the entrepreneur's job, and since he or she can be the only individual with the appropriate authority, it is a necessary area of decision making.

Once the legal form of organization is determined, and the roles necessary to perform all the important functions of the organization are identified, the entrepreneur will need to prepare a job analysis and job descriptions. The job analysis will serve as a guide in determining hiring procedures, training, performance appraisals, compensation programs, as well as job descriptions and specifications. In a very small venture, this process can be simple, but as the size and complexity of the venture grows, the process becomes more complex.

The best place to begin doing job analysis is with the tasks or jobs that need to be performed to make the venture viable. The entrepreneur should prepare a list of necessary tasks and skills. Once a list is completed, the entrepreneur should determine how many positions will be necessary to accomplish these and what type of person or persons would be ideal for each position. Decisions on where to advertise for employees, how they will be trained, who will train them, how they will be evaluated, and how they will be compensated are important in the early stages of organizational planning.

Job Descriptions

The entrepreneur should clarify the roles of employees by preparing *job descriptions.* These job descriptions should specify the details of the work that is to be performed and any special conditions or skills involved in performing the job. Each job description should contain a job summary, the skills or experience required, an outline of the responsibilities and duties, the authority of the individual, and standards of performance. It should be written in clear, direct, simple language. Table 2-1 is an example of a job description for a sales manager.

An entrepreneur also may need to list behavioral traits in a job description. Dave Weignand, president and founder of Advanced Network Design, a telecommunications firm, begins each job description in his company with the activities needed in the job, but then itemizes the behaviors necessary to execute those activities. These behaviors can then be incorporated as questions in the interviewing process. For example, a sales manager's position may require the individual to build confidence in others who face rejection from potential clients and have difficulty making appointments. The only way to determine whether someone fits this requirement is through careful questioning in an interview and asking the candidate for references.

The entrepreneur with no experience may find it difficult writing job descriptions. The most effective method when no direct experience exists is to first outline the needs and objectives of the new venture

Table 2-1. Example job description.

Sales Manager	Requires a BS degree and a minimum of five years, experience in sales and sales management. Responsible for hiring, training, coordinating, and supervising all sales representatives, internal and external to the firm. Monitors sales by territory in the four-state market area. Evaluates marketing programs in the defined territory and provides recommendations with objective to grow sales. Calls on key accounts in market area once every two weeks to provide sales promotion and merchandising support. Prepares annual sales plan for firm, including sales forecasts and goals by territory. Reports to the vice president of marketing and sales.

and then work backward to determine the specific activities that will be needed to achieve these goals. The job descriptions can then be prepared. As the venture grows, these job descriptions may be upgraded or modified to meet the goals and objectives of the firm.

ROLE OF THE BOARD OF DIRECTORS

An entrepreneur should establish a board of directors or board of advisors as early as possible. This board serves a number of functions: (1) reviews operating and capital budgets, (2) develops longer-term strategic plans for growth and expansion, (3) supports day-to-day activities, (4) resolves conflicts among owners and/or shareholders, (5) ensures the proper use of assets, and (6) develops a network of information sources for the entrepreneurs.

Although it is most common to see a board of directors appointed after a venture has been launched, it is helpful to have a board of directors in place earlier and to include the board in the business plan. In this case, the board becomes an important part of the management team and the organization plan when the entrepreneur seeks funding for the new venture. Typically, this board would assist the entrepreneur in day-to-day decision making for either financial remuneration or, more likely, for stock or stock options in the business. As the venture grows, the role of the board changes to considering more strategic, big-picture issues, with the day-to-day decision making now being done by the management team. Since a board's involvement has been shown to be positively related to financial performance, the entrepreneur benefits from having a board of directors as soon as possible.

This external board of directors not only provides important expertise but also adds prestige to the venture, which can be valuable in obtaining investors, establishing supply relationships, or identifying strong potential customers. The members of the board should be carefully selected using the following criteria:

- Select individuals who can work with a diverse group and will commit to the venture's mission.

- Select candidates who understand the market environment or can contribute important skills to the new venture's achievement of planning goals.
- Select candidates who show good judgment in business decision making.
- Select candidates who are extremely bright and competent and will speak out in a board meeting.

Candidates can be identified using referrals from business associates or from any external advisors such as banks, investors, lawyers, accountants, or consultants. Ideally, the board should consist of at least five members with limited terms to allow for continuous infusion of new ideas from different people.

The performance of the board of directors needs to be regularly evaluated. It is the responsibility of the chairperson of the board of directors to provide an appraisal of each board member. In order to provide this appraisal, the chairperson should have a written description of the responsibilities and expectations of board members and should evaluate the contributions of each one.

Compensation for board members can be shares of stock, stock options, or dollar payment. Often the new venture will tie compensation to the performance of the new venture. Compensation is important since it reinforces the responsibility of each board member.

The expert advice and outside perspectives that come from a good board of directors is extremely valuable to the entrepreneur, who probably could not get the same kind of feedback from employees within the firm. Of course, for a board to be effective the entrepreneur must be open to views of people outside the company. There is a lot of time involved in managing a good board. Preparation for a board meeting is important and takes a lot of time in establishing an agenda and making sure all the information is available. The entrepreneur needs to keep board members informed in between meetings as well, particularly in light of the newly passed regulations on the duties of the board and its various committees. Some feel that an entrepreneur/CEO can spend as much as 15 percent of his or her time on board-related issues.

USE OF A BOARD OF ADVISORS

A board of advisors is more loosely tied to the organization and serves the venture in an advisory capacity for some functions or activities. It has no legal status, unlike the board of directors, and hence is not subject to the pressures of fiduciary responsibility and legal liability that occurs with a board of directors. These boards of advisors are likely to meet less frequently, depending on the need, to discuss important venture decisions. A board of advisors is especially useful in a family business, where the board of directors may consist entirely of family members.

A good example of a successful family business that makes good use of an outside board of advisors is Legal Seafoods. At the advice of an attorney, the family formed a five-member, diverse board of advisors that included a dean of a business school, a lawyer, a chemical engineer, a venture capitalist, and the owner of a chain of supermarkets. The board of advisors meets every few months or whenever needed. The family finds that the board of advisors often provides a very different perspective since they are not closely tied to the everyday business activities of the company. For example, the family was debating whether to expand into the New Jersey market. The board of advisors recommended that the family not expand, which solidified the existing doubts that some of the family members had at that time.

The entrepreneur usually will need to use outside advisors such as accountants, bankers, lawyers, advertising agencies, and market researchers on an as-needed basis. These advisors, who are separate from the more formal board of advisors, also can become an important part of the organization and thus will need to be managed, just like any other part of the new venture.

The relationship between the entrepreneur and any outside advisors can be enhanced by seeking out the best advisors and involving them thoroughly at an early stage. Advisors should be assessed or interviewed just as if they were being hired for a permanent position. References should be checked and questions asked to ascertain the quality of the individual, his or her expertise as well as compatibility with the management team.

MAXIMIZING THE BOARD'S EFFECTIVENESS

Whether a board of advisors or directors works well depends on how well it is created and managed. Only the entrepreneur's putting forth the necessary time, effort, and planning will allow a board to fulfill its potential and purpose. One of the biggest problems is meeting management. While it is always useful for employees in the company to get to know the board and the board to get to know them through "show and tell" sessions, these should be a very small part of each board meeting. While members of the board like hearing about the company through its employees, they are not at the meeting to listen—they are at the meeting to share their expertise and experience. The best way to maximize this sharing is to send each board member an information packet at least one week prior to the meeting and give a "homework" assignment. This allows each member to be well informed and be able and ready to contribute to a thorough discussion at the meeting on the topics "assigned" as well as other topics on the agenda.

By establishing good boards and an effective organizational form and structure, the entrepreneur can proceed in the operation of a successful start-up company.

3

Giving Up Control

PROFILE—EWING MARION KAUFFMAN

Born on a farm in Garden City, Missouri, Ewing Marion Kauffman began his career in 1947 as a pharmaceutical salesperson after serving in the Navy during World War II. The job involved selling supplies of vitamins and liver shots to doctors. Working on straight commission, without expenses or benefits, his pay was higher than the president's salary by the end of the second year; the president promptly cut the commission. Eventually, Kauffman was made Midwest sales manager, where he made 3 percent of everything his salespeople sold and continued to make more money than the president. When his territory was cut, he eventually quit and in 1950 started his own company—Marion Laboratories, using his middle name.

When reflecting on founding the new company, Ewing Kauffman commented, "It was easier than it sounds because I had doctors whom I had been selling office supplies to for several years. Before I made the break, I went to three of them and said, 'I'm thinking of starting my own company. May I count on you to give me your orders if I can give you the same quality and service?' These three were my biggest accounts, and each one of them agreed because they liked me and were happy to do business with me."

Marion Laboratories started by marketing injectable products manufactured by another company. The company expanded to other accounts and other products, such as tablets, and then developed its first prescription product, Vicam, a vitamin product. The second pharmaceutical product, oyster shell calcium, also sold well.

In order to expand the company, Kauffman borrowed $5000 from the Commerce Trust Company. He repaid the loan, and the company continued to grow. After several years, outside investors could buy $1000 worth of common stock, if they loaned the company $1000 to be paid back in five years at $1250, without any intermittent interest. This initial $1000 investment, if held until 1993, would have been worth $21 million.

Marion Laboratories continued to grow and reached over $1 billion a year in sales due primarily to the relationship between Mr. Kauffman and the people in the company, who were called associates, not employees. "They are all stockholders, they built this company, and they mean so much to us," said Kauffman. The concept of associates was also a part of the two basic philosophies of the company: those who produce should share in the results or profits, and treat others as you would like to be treated.

The company went public through Smith Barney on August 16, 1965, at $21 per share. The stock jumped to $28 per share immediately and continued to increase, sometimes selling at a 50 to 60 price/earnings multiple. The associates of the company were offered a profit-sharing plan, where each could own stock in the company. When Marion Laboratories merged with Merrell Dow in 1989, there were 3400 associates, 300 of whom became millionaires as a result of the merger.

Ewing Marion Kauffman understood that in order to really be successful he had to learn to give up some control and trust others—his associates. While every business needs a leader with a vision, in today's hypercompetitive environment, things move too quickly, competition is too strong, and the need for specialization too great for a one-person show to survive. Thus an entrepreneur needs to follow Ewing Marion Kauffman's example and learn how to give up control—learn how to be an intrapreneur.

This chapter focuses on solving this problem by (1) establishing an intrapreneurial culture, (2) developing an intrapreneurial climate, (3) developing intrapreneurial leaders, (4) using the Intrapreneurship Formula, (5) developing an intrapreneurial organization, (6) outlining criteria for evaluating intrapreneurial proposals, (7) overcoming barriers to intrapreneurship, and (8) recognizing indicators of an intrapreneurial climate in an organization.

ESTABLISHING AN INTRAPRENEURIAL CULTURE

The typical corporate culture has a climate and reward system that favors conservative decision making. Emphasis is on gathering large amounts of data as the basis for a rational decision and then using that data to justify the decision should the intended results not occur. Risky decisions are often postponed until enough hard facts can be gathered or a consultant hired to "illuminate the unknown." Frequently, there are so many sign-offs and approvals required for a large-scale project that no individual takes ownership or feels personally responsible.

The traditional corporate culture differs significantly from an intrapreneurial culture. The guiding directives in a traditional corporate culture are: (1) adhere to the instructions given, (2) do not make any mistakes, (3) do not fail, (4) do not take the initiative but rather wait for instructions, and (5) stay within your assigned area while protecting your backside. This restrictive environment is not conducive to creativity, flexibility, independence, or risk taking—the guiding principles of intrapreneurs. The goals of an intrapreneurial culture are quite different: (1) to develop visions, goals, and action plans; (2) to be rewarded for actions taken; (3) to suggest, try, and experiment; (4) to create and develop regardless of the area; and (5) to take responsibility and ownership.

As would be expected, these two cultures produce different types of individuals and management styles. While traditional managers are motivated primarily by promotion and typical corporate rewards, entrepreneurs and intrapreneurs thrive on independence and the ability to create. The intrapreneurs expect their performance to be suitably rewarded.

There is a different time orientation in the three groups, with managers emphasizing the short run, entrepreneurs emphasizing the long run, and intrapreneurs focused somewhere in between. Similarly, the primary mode of activity of intrapreneurs falls between the delegation activity of managers and the direct involvement of entrepreneurs. Whereas intrapreneurs and entrepreneurs are moderate risk takers, managers are much more cautious. Protecting one's backside and turf is a way of life for many traditional managers, and risky activities are avoided at almost any cost. On the other hand, most entrepreneurs usually fail at least once, and intrapreneurs learn to conceal risky projects from management until the last possible moment.

Whereas traditional managers tend to be most concerned about those at a higher level in the organization, entrepreneurs serve themselves and their customers, and intrapreneurs add sponsors to these two entrepreneurial categories. This reflects the respective backgrounds of the three types of individuals. Instead of building strong relationships with those around them the way entrepreneurs and intrapreneurs do, traditional managers tend to follow the relationships outlined in the organizational chart. Another aspect of culture that is of concern to businesspeople at all levels is ethics.

CLIMATE FOR INTRAPRENEURSHIP

How can the climate for intrapreneurship be established in an organization? In establishing an intrapreneurial environment, certain factors and leadership characteristics need to be operant. The overall characteristics of a good intrapreneurial environment are summarized in Table 3-1.

The first of these is that the organization operates on the frontiers of technology. Since research and development are key sources for successful new product ideas, the firm must operate on the cutting edge of the industry's technology, encouraging and supporting new

Table 3-1. Intrapreneurial environment.

- Organization operates on frontiers of technology
- New ideas encouraged
- Trial and error encouraged
- Failures allowed
- No opportunity parameters
- Resources available and accessible
- Multidiscipline teamwork approach
- Long time horizon
- Volunteer program
- Appropriate reward system
- Sponsors and champions available
- Support of top management

ideas instead of discouraging them, as frequently occurs in firms that require a rapid return on investment and a high sales volume.

Second, experimentation—trial and error—is encouraged. It took time and some product failures before the first marketable computer appeared. A company wanting to establish an intrapreneurial spirit has to establish an environment that allows mistakes and failures in developing new, innovative products or services. Almost every entrepreneur has experienced at least one failure in his or her life in establishing a successful venture.

Third, an organization should make sure there are no initial opportunity parameters inhibiting creativity. Frequently in an organization, various "turfs" are protected, thereby frustrating attempts by potential intrapreneurs to establish new ventures. In one Fortune 500 company, an attempt to establish an intrapreneurial environment ran into problems and eventually failed when the potential intrapreneurs were informed that a proposed new product was not possible because it was in the domain of another division.

Fourth, the resources of the firm need to be available and easily accessible. As one intrapreneur stated, "If my company really wants me to take the time, effort, and career risks to establish a new venture, then it needs to put money and people resources on the line." Often, insufficient funds are allocated not to creating something new, but instead to solving problems that have an immediate effect on the bottom line. Some companies, like Xerox, 3M, and AT&T, have recognized this problem and have established separate venture capital areas for funding new internal ventures. Even when resources are available, all too often the reporting requirements become obstacles to obtaining them, causing frustration and dissatisfaction.

Fifth, a multidiscipline team approach needs to be encouraged. This open approach, with participation by needed individuals regardless of area, is the antithesis of the typical corporate organizational structure. An evaluation of successful cases of intrapreneurship indicated that one key to success was the existence of "skunkworks" involving a team of relevant people.

Besides encouraging teamwork, the corporate environment must establish a long time horizon for evaluating the success of the overall program as well as the success of each individual venture. If a company is not willing to invest money without an expectation of return for 5 to 10 years, it should not attempt to create an intrapreneurial environment. This patient attitude toward money in the corporate setting is no different from the investment/return line horizon used by venture capitalists and angel investors in the risk-capital market when investing in an entrepreneurial effort.

Sixth, the spirit of intrapreneurship cannot be forced upon individuals, but rather must be fostered on a volunteer basis. There is a difference between corporate thinking and intrapreneurial thinking, with certain individuals performing much better on one side of the continuum or the other. An individual willing to spend the excess hours and effort to create a new venture needs the opportunity and the accompanying reward of completing the project. An intrapreneur falls in love with the newly created product or service or internal venture and will do almost anything to help ensure its success.

The seventh characteristic is a reward system. The intrapreneur needs to be appropriately rewarded for all the energy, effort, and risk expended in the creation of the new venture. These rewards should be based on the attainment of established performance goals.

Eighth, a corporate environment favorable for intrapreneurship has sponsors and champions throughout the organization who not only support the creative activity and resulting failures but also have the planning flexibility to establish new objectives and directions as needed. As one intrapreneur stated, "For a new business venture to succeed, the intrapreneur needs to be able to alter plans at will and not be concerned about how close they come to achieving the previously stated objectives."

Finally, and perhaps most importantly, the intrapreneurial activity must be wholeheartedly supported and embraced by top management, both by physical presence and by making sure that the personnel and the financial resources are readily and easily available. Without top management support, a successful intrapreneurial environment cannot be created in an organization.

INTRAPRENEURIAL LEADERS

Within this overall corporate environment, certain individual characteristics have been identified that constitute a successful intrapreneur. These include understanding the environment, being visionary and flexible, creating management options, encouraging teamwork while employing a multidisciplined approach, encouraging open discussion, building a coalition of supporters, and persisting.

An intrapreneur needs to understand all aspects of the environment. Part of this ability is reflected in the individual's level of creativity. To establish a successful intrapreneurial venture, the individual must be creative and have a broad understanding of the internal and external environments of the corporation.

The person who is going to establish a successful new intrapreneurial venture also must be a visionary leader—a person who dreams great dreams. Although there are many definitions of *leadership*, here is the one that best describes that needed for intrapreneurship: "A leader is like a gardener. When you want a tomato, you take a seed, put it in fertile soil, and carefully water under tender care. You don't manufacture tomatoes, you grow them." Another good definition is that "leadership is the ability to dream great things and communicate these in such a way that people say yes to being a part of the dream." Martin Luther King Jr., said, "I have a dream," and articulated that dream in such a way that thousands followed him in his efforts, in spite of overwhelming obstacles. To establish a successful new venture, the intrapreneurial leader must have a dream and overcome all the obstacles in achieving it by selling the dream to others.

The third necessary characteristic is that the intrapreneur must be flexible and create management options. An intrapreneur does not "mind the store," but rather is open to and even encourages change. By challenging the beliefs and assumptions of the corporation, an intrapreneur has the opportunity to create something new in the organizational structure.

The intrapreneur must possess a fourth characteristic—the ability to encourage teamwork and use a multidisciplined approach. In forming a new venture, recruiting those in the organization usually requires crossing established departmental structure and reporting systems. To minimize the negative effect of any disruption caused, the intrapreneur must be a good diplomat.

Open discussion needs to be encouraged in order to develop a good team for creating something new. Many corporate managers have forgotten the frank, open discussions and disagreements that were a part of their educational process. Instead, they spend time building protective barriers and insulating themselves. A successful new intrapreneurial venture can be formed only when the team involved feels the freedom to disagree and to critique an idea in an effort to reach the best solution. The degree of openness among the team depends on the degree of openness of the intrapreneur.

Openness also leads to the establishment of a strong coalition of supporters and encouragers. The intrapreneur must encourage and affirm each team member, particularly during difficult times. This encouragement is very important, as the usual motivators of career paths and job security are not operational in establishing a new intrapreneurial venture. A good intrapreneur makes everyone a hero.

Last, but not least, is persistence. Throughout the establishment of any new intrapreneurial venture, frustration and obstacles will occur. Only through the intrapreneur's persistence will a new venture be created and successful commercialization result.

ESTABLISHING INTRAPRENEURSHIP IN THE ORGANIZATION

An organization desiring to establish an intrapreneurial environment must implement a procedure. Although this can be done internally, frequently it is easier to use someone from the outside to facilitate the process. This is particularly true when the organization's existing environment is very traditional and has a record of little change and few new products being introduced in the last several years.

The first step in this process is to secure a commitment to intrapreneurship in the organization at all levels—top, upper, and middle management. Without this, the organization will never be able to go through all the cultural changes necessary for establishing an intrapreneurial environment. Once the top management of the organization has committed to intrapreneurship for a sufficient period of time (1 to 3 years), the concept is introduced throughout the organization. This is accomplished most effectively through seminars, where the aspects of intrapreneurship are introduced and strategies are developed to transform the organizational culture into an intrapreneurial one. General guidelines need to be established for intrapreneurial venture development. Once the initial framework is established and the concept embraced, intrapreneurial leaders need to be identified, selected, and trained. This training needs to focus on obtaining resources within the organization, identifying viable opportunities and their markets, and developing the appropriate business plan.

Second, ideas and general areas that top management are most interested in supporting should be identified, along with the amount of risk money that is available to develop the concept further. Overall program expectations and the target results of each intrapreneurial venture should be established. As much as possible, these should specify the time frame, volume, and profitability requirements for the new venture, and the impact of the organization. Along with the intrapre eurial training, a mentor/sponsor system needs to be established.

Third, a company needs to use technology to make itself more flexible. For the past decade, small companies have successfully used technology to put them on a level playing field with larger firms. How else could a small firm like Value Quest Ltd. compete against very large money management firms except through a state-of-the-art personal computer and access to large data banks? Similarly, large companies can use technology to make themselves responsive and flexible like smaller firms.

Fourth, the organization can foster an intrapreneurial culture by using a group of interested managers to train and share their experiences. The training sessions should be conducted one day per month. Informational items about intrapreneurship in general and about the specifics of the company's activities in developing ideas into marketable products or services that are the basis of new business venture units should be well publicized.

Fifth, the organization needs to develop ways to get closer to its customers. By tapping the database, hiring from smaller rivals, and helping the retailer, a company can establish more personal relationships with those with whom they do business. Pepsi Co., Inc., spent about $20 million to create electronic profiles of about 9 million Pizza Hut customers. Dannon shared its research with retailers and tailored much of its marketing effort to the individual chains.

Sixth, an organization that wants to become more intrapreneurial must learn to be more productive with fewer resources. Top-heavy organizations are out of date in today's hypercompetitive environment. To accommodate the large cutbacks, much more control has to be given to subordinates at all levels in the organization. Not surprisingly, the span of control may become as high as 30 to 1 in divisions of some companies. The concept of "lean and mean" needs to exist if intrapreneurship is to prevail.

Seventh, the organization needs to establish a strong support structure for intrapreneurship. This is particularly important, since intrapreneurship is usually a secondary activity in the organization. Since intrapreneurial activities do not immediately affect the bottom line, they easily can be overlooked and receive little funding and support.

Eighth, the support also must involve tying the rewards to the performance of the intrapreneurial unit. This encourages the team members to work harder and compete more effectively, since they will benefit directly from their efforts.

Finally, the organization needs to implement an evaluation system that allows successful intrapreneurial units to expand and unsuccessful ones to be eliminated. Just as it occurs in an entrepreneurial firm, when a good job is done, an intrapreneurial unit should be allowed to expand to fill market demands as warranted. The organization can establish constraints to ensure that this expansion does not run contrary to the corporate mission statement. To have a successful intrapreneurial environment, the organization must allow some ventures to fail even as it allows more successful ones to expand.

FORMULA FOR INTRAPRENEURSHIP

Based on many consulting assignments and research on intrapreneurship, the following formula has become the basis for establishing an intrapreneurial culture and climate in an organization:

Intrapreneurship = COC^2
Where C = Creativity
O = Ownership
C = Change
C = Commitment

Empowering your employees to be creative is the first C of the formula. The more the bureaucracy operating in a company, the more difficult it is to encourage people in your organization to be creative. A typical organization has an established culture that makes it difficult for an employee at any level to develop and then implement a creative new way of doing things, particularly if this involves a radical new procedure or way of thinking. A typical organizational culture gives precise instructions on how things are to be done instead of sharing the vision and goals of the organization and allowing employees and managers to creatively find the best way to obtain optimal results. The traditional management techniques of stability, predictability, planability, and certainty minimize the opportunity for any creative new way of doing things or any potential new products or services being formulated and implemented. An intrapreneurial culture supports, protects, and advises employees while sharing the vision for the organization so that individuals will take ownership of the vision and their actions.

Ownership is the next element of the formula. When ownership is present in an organization, employees at all levels feel empowered to make decisions and then stand behind them. The bureaucratic fear of making a mistake and failing—the fail environment—is gone and so is the overall threat of punishing those responsible. These fears are replaced by employees being encouraged to make a decision, to try something that might lead to the next step, and being rewarded for actions taken—a success environment. By having an environment that tolerates mistakes and internal competition, individuals in the organization are stimulated to be creative and actively think about and develop new ideas and take the risks in doing this. This allows a company to continually develop new products and services and have at the very least 20 percent of the sales come from products and services introduced in the last 5 years.

Change—the next C in the formula—is essential to any organization not only being intrapreneurial but also being successful. In previous eras of less global competition and a slower-moving technological environment, the key phrase was, "If it ain't broke, don't fix it," indicating that change occurred infrequently and when it did occur, it occurred incrementally. By any measure, the amount of significant change in an organization has grown significantly over the past two decades. Given the hypercompetitive environment and the powerful macroeconomic focus at work, it is doubtful that this rapid rate of change will diminish in the next two decades and probably will even accelerate. This will result in all successful organizations finding new opportunities for growth, increasing productivity, improving the quality of their products and services, focusing on the customer and customer satisfaction, and reducing costs. Since every successful organization will need to change, particularly those wanting to create an intrapreneurial environment, knowledge of how such change can be successfully implemented must be evident. In other words, how can an organization be transformed? One way is to follow the nine-stage process indicated in Figure 3-1. The nine stages of the process help avoid most of the errors that undermine the transformation process. The steps are (1) establishing a sense of urgency, (2) forming a powerful guiding coalition, (3) creating a vision of the end result, (4) communicating the vision, (5) selecting a champion, (6) empowering others to act on the vision, (7) planning for and creating short-term wins,

1	**Establish a Sense of Urgency** • Examining market and competitive realties • Identifying and discussing crises, potential crises, or opportunities • Develop appropriate guidelines for time frame • Implementation must be achievable within the existing scope of organizational resources
2	**Forming a Powerful Guiding Coalition** • Assembling a group with enough power to lead the change effort • Encouraging and allowing the group to work together as a team • Organize a team of established leaders who can implement and obtain buy-in of others and also work toward organizational goals without blocking tasks with personal agendas
3	**Creating a Vision of End Result** • Creating a vision to help direct the change effort • Developing a strategic plan (mission, goals/objectives, strategies/tactics) for achieving that vision
4	**Communicating the Vision** • Using every vehicle possible to communicate the new vision and strategies • Teaching new behaviors by example of the guiding coalition • Measuring progress toward the end goal must be visible and continually communicated to all
5	**Selecting a Champion** • Selecting a champion that can spearhead the transformation • Champion needs to be able to communicate the vision in a powerful way
6	**Empowering Others to Act on the Vision** • Getting rid of obstacles to change • Changing systems that undermine the vision and discourage risk taking • Rewarding creative thinking and implementation at any level • Acknowledge that employees are the ones responsible for achieving success
7	**Planning For and Creating Short-Term Wins** • Planning for visible performance improvements • Recognizing and rewarding employees involved in the improvements with more than token rewards • Stair-step achievements: Winning small battles to "win the war" • Build in accomplishments which lead to the end goal and reward those that add value to that achievement
8	**Consolidating Improvements and Producing Still More Changes** • Using increased credibility to change systems, structures, and policies • Hiring, promoting, and developing employees who can implement the vision • Giving employees the opportunity to initiate changes
9	**Institutionalizing New Approaches** • Articulating the connections between new behaviors and success • Developing the means to ensure leadership development and succession • Standardizing the process for all future change initiatives

Adapted from: John P. Kotter, "Leading change: why transformation efforts fail," *Harvard Business Review* (March-April 1995), pp. 59–62.

Figure 3-1. Nine steps to transforming your organization.

(8) consolidating improvements and producing more changes, and (9) institutionalizing the new approaches into the culture of the organization. The first four steps help soften a hardened status quo which has resisted change up to this point in time. Even organizations that have not been rigid in the last decade need to undertake these four steps, as change is not easy and resistance will be met somewhere in the firm. While steps 5 through 8 introduce new practices, step 9 anchors the new approaches into the corporate culture so that change is always present. Since most major change initiatives are composed of a number of smaller projects, each of which also goes through a multistage process, at any one time an organization in change might be halfway through the overall change effort, finished with one smaller piece, three-quarters of the way through another smaller piece, and just beginning other pieces.

The final C in the formula is commitment. A majority of the managerial team and particularly the head of the organization must be committed to facilitating intrapreneurship for at least 5 years. It will take at least this long for the organization to realize any benefits such as cost reduction, increased productivity, better morale, and more new products or services being developed. This commitment will lead to a new model being apparent in the organization—suggest, try, and experiment; do not wait for instructions. Management will tolerate disorder and ambiguity and encourage individuals in the organization to experiment and test. The culture will be one of trusting people and not interfering. The job becomes one of getting the task done, not working from 8 to 4 or 9 to 5. Going to work is not a chore, it is fun.

CRITERIA FOR EVALUATING PROPOSALS

Two critical issues in successfully establishing an intrapreneurial environment relate to evaluating the proposals and establishing the right reward system. In establishing criteria for evaluating the proposals, it is important that everyone knows the criteria being used as well as the evaluation process. Any hint of "smoke and mirrors" must be removed so that the process is impartial and fair to all. It is a good idea to

Table 3-2. Corporate venture planning guide.

Corporate venture planning guide
Executive Summary
Corporate fit
Product fit into corporate goals
Customer base
Utilization of assets
Staff needs
Effect on business community
Product/Service analysis
Purpose of the product/service
Stage of development
Product limitation
Proprietary rights
Governmental approvals
Product liability
Related services and spin-offs
Production
Market analysis
Current market size
Growth potential of the market
Industry trends
Competition profile
Customer profile
Customer benefits
Target markets
Market penetration
Price and profitability
Price list
Sales estimate
Cost of product/service
Gross margin
Three-year operating expenses
Three-year operating statement
Start-up costs
Capital expenditures
Plan for further action
Pitfalls
Positives
Needed capital
Role of corporate venture manager
Business plan
License potential
Corporate partners
Proprietary rights
Corporate staff
Corporate venturing executive board

establish a corporate venture planning guide, such as the one shown in Table 3-2, and make available example plans as well as those plans that were successful.

Certain criteria are important in evaluating intrapreneurial proposals and selecting the ones that have the highest probability of being successful. These criteria include a high degree of corporate fit, low initial investment, an experienced venture champion, experience with the proposed new product/service, low competitive threat, proprietary technology, high gross margin, and a high rate of return. These criteria are reflected in the characteristics of an ideal intrapreneurial new venture as shown in Table 3-3. Since characteristics such as no investment or 100 percent gross margin can probably never be fully met, the ideal new venture should come as close to as many of these characteristics important to the particular organization as possible.

Table 3-3. Characteristics of an ideal intrapreneurial new venture.

- No investment
- Recognized, established market
- Perceived need for product
- Dependable source of input supply
- No government regulation
- No labor
- 100 percent gross margin
- Buyers purchase frequently
- Favorable tax treatment
- Receptive, established distribution system
- Business with great news value
- Customers pay in advance
- No product- or service-liability risk
- No product obsolescence
- No competition
- No fashion obsolescence
- No physical perishability
- Impervious to weather
- Product/service is workable and feasible
- Proprietary rights
- Continuous revenue flow
- No legal entanglements
- Exit potential

INDICATORS OF AN INTRAPRENEURIAL CLIMATE

These barriers should not deter organizations from committing to intrapreneurship and starting the process for establishing an intrapreneurial culture. There are numerous examples of companies that, having understood the environmental and intrapreneurial characteristics necessary, have adopted their own version of the implementation process previously discussed to launch new ventures successfully. One of the best known of these firms is Minnesota Mining and Manufacturing (3M). Having had many successful intrapreneurial efforts, 3M in effect allows employees to devote 15 percent of their time to independent projects. This enables the divisions of the company to meet an important goal: that a significant percent of sales come from new products introduced within the last 5 years. One of the most successful of these intrapreneurial activities was the development of Post-It Notes by intrapreneur Arthur Fry. This effort developed out of Fry's annoyance that pieces of paper marking his church hymnal constantly fell out while he was singing. As a 3M chemical engineer, Fry knew about the discovery by a scientist, Spencer Silver, of a very-low-sticking-power adhesive, which to the company was a poor product characteristic. However, this characteristic was perfect for Fry's problem; a marker with lightly sticking adhesive that is easy to remove provided a good solution. Obtaining approval to commercialize the idea proved to be a monumental task until the samples distributed to secretaries within 3M, as well as other companies, created such a demand that the company eventually began selling the product under the name Post-It. Sales have reached more than $800 million.

Another firm committed to the concept of intrapreneurship is Hewlett-Packard (HP). After failing to recognize the potential of Steven Wozniak's proposal for a personal computer (which was the basis for Apple Computer Inc.), Hewlett-Packard has taken steps to ensure that it will be recognized as a leader in innovation and not miss future opportunities. However, the intrapreneurial road at HP is not an easy one. This was the case for Charles House, an engineer who went far beyond his intrapreneurial duty when he ignored an order from David Packard to stop working on a high-quality video monitor. The monitor, once developed, was used in heart transplants and in NASA's manned moon landings. Although projected to achieve sales of no more than 30 units, more than 17,000 of these large-screen displays (about $35 million in sales) have already been sold.

IBM also decided that intrapreneurship would help spur corporate growth. The company developed the independent business unit concept in which each unit is a separate organization, with its own miniboard of directors and autonomous decision-making authority on many manufacturing and marketing issues. The more than 11 business units have developed such products as the automatic teller machine for banks, industrial robots, and the IBM personal computer. The latter business unit was given a blank check with a mandate to get IBM into the personal computer market. Intrapreneur Philip Estridge led his group to develop and market the PCs, through both IBM's sales force and the retail market, breaking some of the most binding operational rules of IBM at that time.

These and other success stories indicate that the problems of intrapreneurship are not insurmountable and that the concept can lead to new products, growth, and the development of an entirely new corporate environment and culture.

How can one ascertain whether an intrapreneurial culture has developed? There are many indicators of this, which should be benchmarked before the process is started and then reassessed periodically. Some of these indicators include self-selection; no hand-offs; the doer decides; corporate slack; home-run philosophy; degree of tolerance of risk, failures, and mistakes; amount of patient money; freedom from turf wars; the number of cross-functional teams; and the percent of sales and profits coming from products and services introduced in the last 5 years.

By giving up autonomous control and establishing an intrapreneurial climate in a company, a successful business venture can be created and profits realized.

4

Attracting and Retaining Employees

PROFILE—BRIAN FARRELL—THQ

Started in 1990 in Colobases Hills, California, THQ licenses, finances, and markets video games designed by other companies. When Brian Farrell became chairman and chief executive officer in 1995 the company started focusing more on creating its own video games for distribution, which required recruiting some very creative talent. This was a very difficult task, as the company was not perceived as the best creative game developer. In fact, it did not have a good reputation in the industry. How does a small innovative company attract good, highly creative employees? By emphasizing its smaller size and the fact that the company allowed much more creative freedom than could be found elsewhere. Instead of being one project in a thousand at a company such as Electronic Arts or Sega Corp., a project at THQ in developing a great game would be noticed and given recognition and greater responsibility.

Another advantage of working at THQ used in attracting the best creative talent was that the programmers and graphic designers could work on a spectrum of games instead of working on the same type of games every year, as is often the case for employees at large game makers. In large game developers, an employee usually works on the same game year after year making small incremental advances on each new game generation. THQ, instead, allows choice of games and projects in its creative-nurturing culture.

To ensure that it retains this creative, free atmosphere the company makes sure the creative workers are not in close proximity or share the same office. In fact, the creative staff of the company is housed in creative studios throughout the United States in such cities as Boston, Los Angeles, and Seattle, another positive feature used in attracting key employees. This also allows the company to tap any specialized creative talent in the region surrounding that particular city.

It is not only the environment to be creative and the ability to work on a wide variety of products that is attractive to potential employees, but also that THQ offers a competitive salary and a royalty structure that allows those who work on a hit game to share the rewards of its successful sales and therefore earn a great deal of money. With the royalties (bonuses) linked to the sales of the particular games, the bonuses can amount to two to three times the employee's base salary, depending on the sales success of the game.

The company also offers stock options that vest over 4 years. This gives the employees an equity upside and significantly helps in retention, as it makes it difficult for an employee to leave before the end of the vesting period.

The recruitment and retention strategy is working. Although the stock of THQ is down about two-thirds from its December 2002 value, the stock has the potential to significantly increase as the market capitalization of the company has grown from under $8 million in 1995 to over $600 million today.

A cult of personality has in recent years built up around the entrepreneur, and the success of the entire business is perceived to be the work of a single person. Similar to THQ, every entrepreneurial business has some key jobs that provide key support for the business. Sometimes this is the technical manager marshalling the creative talent into coming up with and developing successful new products. Sometimes it is the financial manager, who understands and monitors the costs and reduces the cash cycle so that the business does not run out of cash. Or, maybe it is the sales manager who really understands the market and develops and implements the optimal marketing plan for successful sales. Or maybe it is all three.

For a small entrepreneurial business, the difficulty and importance of obtaining and retaining good employees is one key to success and a big mistake to avoid. Attracting and retaining talented employees, the focus of this chapter, can be the difference between success and failure.

COMPENSATION

Given the hypercompetition, the need for shareholder value, and economic turbulence in today's business climate, it is important that each entrepreneur construct the appropriate compensation package for his or her employees. Compensation is more than just money, whether it is paid in wages, salaries, commissions, or bonuses. Other forms of extrinsic compensation include equity; stock options; perquisites, such as a company car; child care; expense account; membership privileges; health care; personal insurance; and pension contribution. Extending the term *compensation* to the fullest would include such intrinsic compensation as status; independence; power; office; company parking place; type of office furnishings and computer; vacations and holidays; and family, personal, and sick leave. Compensation options are listed in Figures 4-1 and 4-2. Analysis of related factors is provided in Table 4-1. Using these three items, the entrepreneur can develop a compensation package consisting of economic and noneconomic aspects for each employee or employee group and then, most importantly, review this with the employee(s) on an annual basis.

Smaller entrepreneurial firms generally provide fewer and different benefits than larger firms. While this reflects the size of the business, it also is a result of the fact that most smaller firms are less likely to be unionized. One cause of this difference is the substantial overhead cost of benefit administration, which could include having

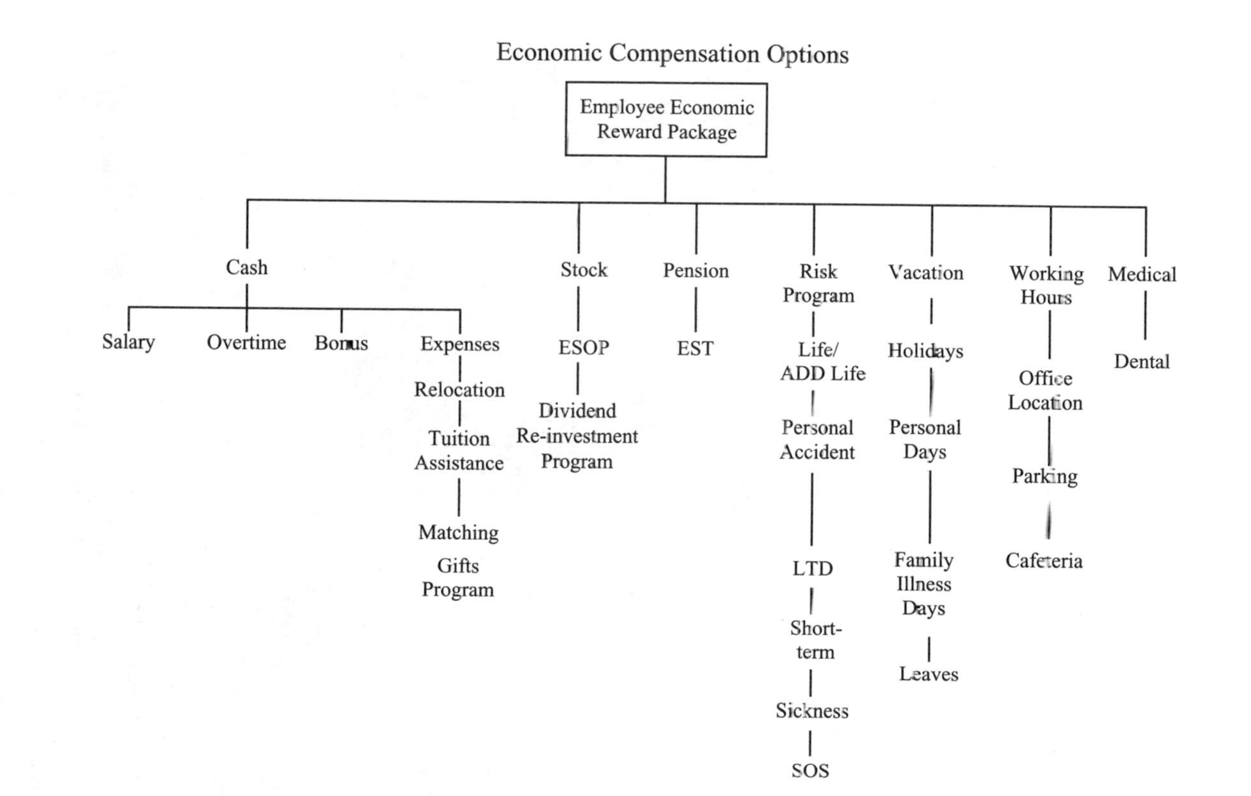

Figure 4-1. Compensation options: Employee economic reward package.
Source: Adapted from material of Gerard Torma, Director of Compensation and International Human Resources, Nordson Corporation.

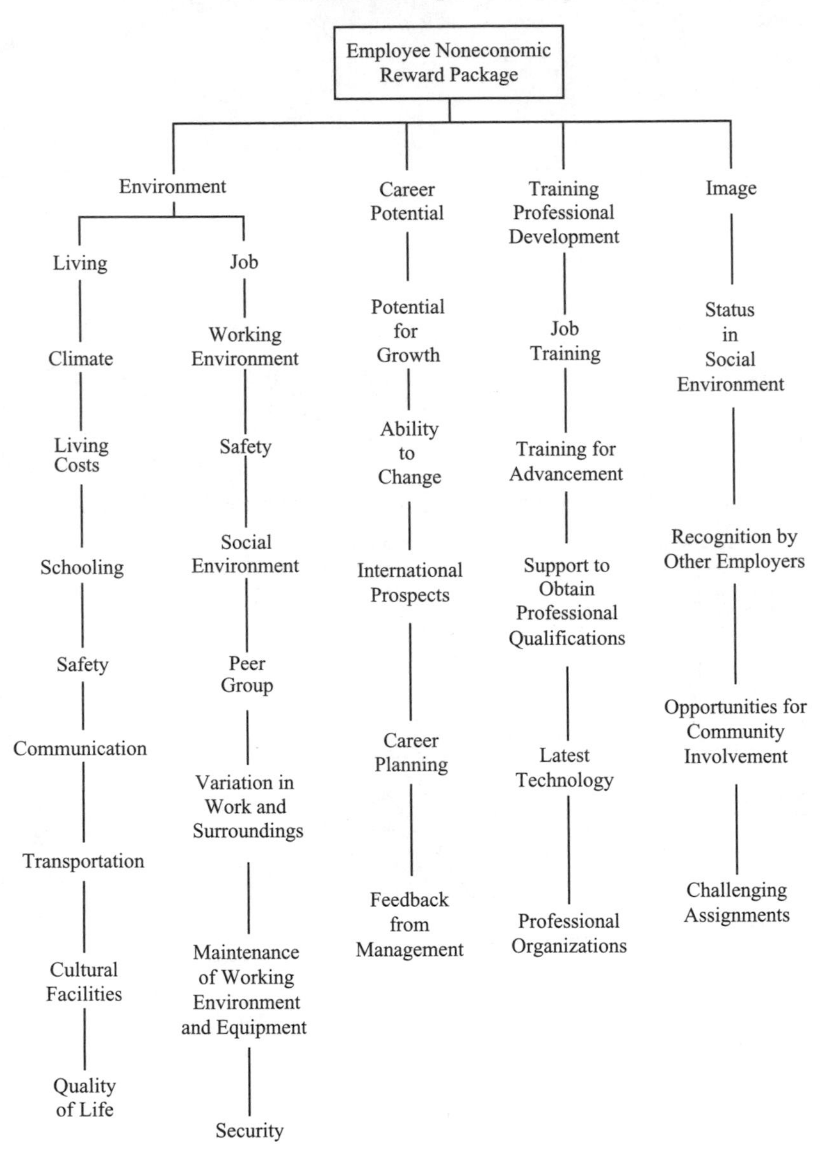

Figure 4-2. Compensation options: Employee noneconomic reward package.
Source: Adapted from material of Gerard Torma, Director of Compensation and International Human Resources, Nordson Corporation.

Table 4-1. Employee compensation analysis.

Factors Affecting Impact of Employee Compensation Packages
• Management style
• Ability to participate
• Employee communications
• Recognition of contribution
• Financial health of corporation
• Market leadership position

Source: Adapted from material of Gerard Torma, Director of Compensation and International Human Resources, Nordson Corporation.

a benefits administrator or a human resource manager on the company's payroll. Since these personnel costs can be amortized over the entire employee base, it takes a certain organizational size in terms of the number of employees to make having a human resource manager and/or benefit administrator to be cost effective.

MONEY AND MOTIVATION

While there is nothing new about using incentives to motivate workers, shareholder mistrust and economic turbulence have caused the shift in motivational leadership to a variety of incentive/pay-for-performance plans. In the extreme case, this makes every employee's compensation a variable cost dependent on his or her productivity and the successful performance of the company. This type of compensation system tends to keep fixed costs low and motivates employees to achieve greater productivity.

Types of Incentive Plans

There are many types of incentive plans that can be classified in several ways. They can be classified by level, with the individual compensation plans providing income to individual employees over and above their base salary when specific individual performance goals are met. If the level is not individual, then it is a group incentive plan, which pays all members in the group or team when the performance goals/standards established for the group are met. Profit-sharing plans provide all or almost all employees with a share of the company's profits in a specific period of time. There are also employee group plans such as those for sales employees, operating employees, or distribution employees.

Incentives for Nonmanagerial Employees

Almost all entrepreneurs employ some individuals who are nonmanagerial and actually perform the operational work of the company. These can include the janitor who cleans the offices, the production worker who makes the product, the receptionist who handles a variety of company tasks, or the data processing clerk who inputs the orders. There are several types of incentive plans that can be used for this type of employment.

Salaried Hour Plan

The salaried hour plan is the most common plan used for nonmanagerial employees. Under this plan an employee is paid a basic hourly rate and an extra percentage of his or her rate for output exceeding the standard. If Sally, a sales lead specialist, is paid $80/per day for getting 40 new leads and she obtains 60 new leads one day, her pay would be $80 + (50% × $80) or $120 that day. Care must be taken by the entrepreneur using this plan that quality is not sacrificed for the quantity that results in increased pay.

Piecework Plan

In the widely used piecework plan, an employee is paid an amount, called a piece rate, for each unit produced. If Sam receives $1.25 for each email sales lead found, he would receive $100 for obtaining

80 leads in one day. The difficult problem for the entrepreneur to implement a piecework plan is determining the correct rate to pay per piece. In the case of Sam in the above example, the entrepreneur felt that Sam's job was worth $10/hour and that 8 good leads per hour was a good standard product rate, therefore a piece rate of $1.25 ($10/hour divided by 8) was established.

The piecework can be either straight or shared depending on the desires of the entrepreneur. The previous case was an example of straight piecework as there is a strict relationship between results and rewards. If shared piecework is used and Sam continually obtains 100 leads per day instead of the 80, which was the initial standard, then his piece rate for leads above 90 might be $1.35.

A piecework compensation plan is very understandable and equitable, and it provides good incentives for employees, as rewards are proportionate to performance. However, this compensation plan can lead to some employee rigidity in terms of resisting improving or even meeting quality standards and not being interested in switching to another job as this may reduce output. The plan also increases resistance to any job change, including using new technology.

Team (Group) Incentive Plans

Team (group) incentive plans reward the team for its performance, from which each team member's pay is derived. The members of the team are paid based on each team member receiving pay equal to the average pay earned by the group or each member receiving the same pay earned by either the highest paid or lowest paid member of the team. Instead of being based on pay, another individual compensation method is to set an engineered production standard; each member of the team then receives the same pay based on the piece rate of output of the team. If you want to avoid using an engineered standard, then the entrepreneur should tie the rewards of the team, and hence the individual, to goals reached based on some overall standard such as the number of defective products and/or number of labor hours per product. This latter plan usually produces great results as the team members are motivated to achieve greater and greater efficiencies determined by management without the use of an engineered standard, which team members usually disagree with.

Generally, team incentives work very well for motivating nonmanagement employees when the work is organized around teams. This type of incentive reinforces team planning and problem solving while helping build *espirit de corps* and collaboration among team members. The entrepreneur should make sure, when using a team incentive plan, that no individual(s) becomes disgruntled because he or she is "carrying" the team, resulting in rewards and pay not proportionate to his or her efforts.

Incentives for Salespeople

Incentives for salespeople are some of the most important incentives to establish, as salespeople drive the top line of the company. As the age-old adage states: "Nothing happens until a sale is made." Sales compensation plans tend to be of three types: straight commission, straight salary plan, or a combination of salary and commissions.

Straight Commission

The straight commission compensation plan maximizes incentives, minimizes security, and frequently results in very high productivity and earning levels for salespeople. This plan is usually employed in direct marketing, some industrial sales, retail furniture sales, automotive sales, international sales of the company's local salespeople selling in their country's market, real estate transactions, and group sales. Under this plan, unproductive salespeople eventually resign because their salaries are derived from paid commissions based only on performance, as measured in terms of sales and sometimes profits or a combination of sales and profits.

When establishing a straight commission plan, the company first must establish the base or unit. This becomes the basis for paying commissions, and is usually stated in units of sale, dollar sales, gross profits, or some sales/profit combination. Second, the company must determine the rate that will be paid per unit, which is often expressed as a percentage of gross profit or sales. Third, the company must establish the starting point for commissions. This point can be the first unit sold, the first unit sold after obtaining a specific level of sales, or an established quota. Finally, the company must decide on the time period for payment of commissions, as well as the method for handling sales returns, canceled orders, and nonpayments.

Commissions are usually paid when the order is received, goods are shipped, or payment is received. Commissions often are adjusted in the next payment period for any nonpayments, canceled orders, or returned merchandize in the previous period. To help ensure prompt delivery and build customer relations, most companies usually pay commissions once the order is shipped. Under this system, salespeople work with production and shipping to ensure that the order is sent on a timely basis, and is not canceled due to delay.

To help offset fluctuations in salary, and to help salespeople on straight commission, some companies provide a draw, in addition to the established commission plan. A draw is a sum of money paid to salespeople against future commissions. The "drawn" money is deducted from commissions earned in the next payment period.

With or without a guaranteed draw, straight commission plans are used in many industries, particularly when the company wants a strong incentive to sell. Some industries, such as consumer packaged goods, tend not to use a straight commission plan because of the difficulty in relating sales volume to the efforts of a particular salesperson. For example, the sale of a 96-ounce box of Ultra Tide at a Giant Eagle store in Cleveland, Ohio, might have been the result of a manufacturer's coupon from Procter & Gamble, not the work of the salesperson calling on the account. It also may have resulted from a call by the sales manager at Giant Eagle's headquarters, a display allowance given by Procter & Gamble to the Giant Eagle store for displaying the product, a product advertisement in the Cleveland *Plain Dealer*, or the salesperson's call on the manager of another Giant Eagle store in the area. In all likelihood, a combination of several of these activities affected the sale.

Straight Salary Plan

Even though individuals with good selling ability are better rewarded (if they can perform) under a straight commission plan, many people do not like to work under conditions of uncertainty and potential for wide fluctuations in income. These more security-minded salespeople prefer a dependable, regular income rather than making a larger amount of money under the uncertain straight commission plan. Security with a straight salary plan is particularly important in widely fluctuating company and market situations and when the company's sales are periodic or seasonal.

A company should definitely consider a straight salary plan under the following circumstances, even though the incentive for higher sales volume may be reduced:

1. When a long learning period is needed for salespeople to perform effectively. A straight salary is needed, at least in the beginning, to cover the training period until commissions are large enough to provide an adequate standard of living. Initially, without a straight salary plan, it would be very difficult to recruit good salespeople.
2. When a major capital expenditure is involved with an extended negotiation period in the selling process. A company may take more than a year to make such a big decision. A salesperson might be calling on, and working with, a company during this entire period in order to make the final sale, and yet would not earn any commission during that time.
3. When sales, usually more technical in nature, require team selling among such people as a salesperson, a marketing support person, a technical engineer, and an upper-level manager. Because each individual plays a role in the final sale, it is difficult to assign total credit to the salesperson.
4. When advertising, sales promotion, and/or a direct-mail piece have a significant effect on the final sale, and when

> the extent of that effect with respect to the efforts of the salesperson is difficult to evaluate. A straight salary plan in this case also rewards nonselling activities, commonly called *missionary selling*. These include providing customer assistance, setting up in-store displays, redesigning an entire area of a store for introducing a new line of products, or calling on potential new customers.

Because a salesperson's compensation in a straight salary plan in not based on productivity, which is usually measured by sales and/or profits, this compensation plan provides salespeople with the most security and allows the company to direct all the sales activities. This helps to ensure that the company will reach its established objectives. In industries such as heavy machinery, aerospace, chemical, petroleum, and consumer nondurable goods, a straight salary compensation plan is widely used. Sometimes salespeople are even called consultants or engineers, with sales not even being a part of their title.

Combination Compensation Plans

A combination compensation plan integrates characteristics of both the straight salary and straight commission plans. The salary part of the compensation package provides security and a base reward for minimal level of sales performance. The commission and/or bonus part of the compensation package is reward for achieving or exceeding volume and/or profit goals. The critical factor in developing an effective combination compensation plan is the proportion of salary to commission incentive. The ideal combination is a salary large enough to attract talented salespeople coupled with an incentive plan large enough to strongly motivate them. Although the salary-incentive mix varies depending on the industry, the competition, and the nature of the selling task, a compensation package that is 70 to 80 percent salary and 20 to 30 percent incentive is usually considered balanced and attractive.

Incentives for Managers and Executives

Probably no other area is more important for the success of the entrepreneur and the business than is attracting and retaining key managers and executives. Since these individuals influence directly the overall performance in terms of sales and profits of the company, the entrepreneur needs to put considerable thought into how to reward them. Most managers receive both short-term bonuses and long-term incentives in addition to their salary.

Short-Term Incentives

Most firms have annual bonus plans designed to motivate the short-term performance of managers and executives; these bonuses are tied to the profitability of the company. Short-term bonuses can significantly adjust pay, sometimes up to 30 percent or more of the total pay received. In establishing the annual bonus or any other short-term incentive plan the entrepreneur needs to keep in mind three things: eligibility, total size of the reward, and individual awards. In terms of eligibility, it is usually better to have as much eligibility as makes sense, including both upper- and lower-level managers. This eligibility can be decided in a number of ways, but it is usually best to determine it based either on job level (title) or a combination of factors such as job level (title), base salary level, and discretionary considerations such as jobs that are key to the company's performance. The size of the bonus received usually varies by job level (title), with top-level executives receiving a higher percentage bonus than a lower-level manager.

The entrepreneur also must decide the total amount of bonus money available—the size of the bonus pool. Entrepreneurs make this decision in several different ways. Some entrepreneurs use a straight percentage (usually of the company's net income) to create the bonus pool. This is called a *nondeductible formula approach*. Other entrepreneurs feel that the bonus pool should be based on amounts achieved only after a certain specified level of earnings are achieved. This is called a *deductible formula approach*. Still other entrepreneurs do not use a formula but determine the size of the bonus pool on some discretionary basis. While there are no hard and fast rules for determining the proportion of the profits to pay out through the bonus pool, the entrepreneur should make this determination carefully so that both managers and shareholders are rewarded and the company can continue to perform and grow.

The third task in developing a good annual bonus plan is deciding the individual awards. Usually an entrepreneur establishes a target bonus and a maximum bonus (usually twice the size of the target bonus) for each eligible position, and the actual individual bonus received reflects the individual's performance. To implement this, the entrepreneur must establish a process for computing the performance ratings of each manager; the preliminary total bonus estimates; the total amount of money required with the total bonus fund available; and then, if applicable, any necessary adjustments to each individual's bonus. While there are no hard and fast rules, usually top-level executives' bonuses are tied to overall company results rather than individual performance, while at the lower levels of management individual performance affects the bonus paid.

Long-Term Incentives

Long-term incentives are used to make sure decisions are made that will impact the long-term (not just the short-term) results of the company and to encourage managers and executives to stay with the company by letting these individuals accumulate capital that can only be cashed in after a specified number of years of employment, the vesting period. In terms of long-term incentives the entrepreneur can use cash, stock, stock appreciation rights, and stock options. Since long-term incentives are so important and are now being scrutinized and reviewed by the legislature in the United States, various stock option plans will be discussed under a separate section of this chapter, called "Equity-Based Compensation."

The long-term incentives have such a profound impact on the strategic success of the company that the entrepreneur should use them over a long period of time to reward managers and executives for contributing to the success of the business. This requires that the entrepreneur first define the company's strategy and then create the compensation package that will reward managers for carrying out this strategy.

EQUITY-BASED COMPENSATION

Smart entrepreneurs recognize that talented people are indispensable to the success of their business and design compensation packages that will attract and retain key employees without overextending the company's resources. Since oftentimes the salary levels needed are beyond the capacity of the firm, equity in the company has become the currency allowing the entrepreneur to compete for the key individual needed. In addition to attracting and retaining key employees, equity-based compensation serves other purposes. It reduces cash flow and book expenses. It minimizes and postpones certain tax liabilities of the company. And, most importantly, it helps employees be concerned about and focus on improving the value of the company.

Stock Options

By far the most popular equity incentive used by entrepreneurs is stock options. A stock option gives the employee the right to buy stock in the company at a stated price (the exercise price) for a specified period of time (option term). When granting a stock option the company presently does not take any charge to earnings (although this law may change due to increasing legislative interest following several scandalous company situations such as Enron, Worldcom, and Adelphia Cable). The company also realizes positive cash flow when the option is exercised (turned in for stock) while obtaining loyalty to the company from individuals critical to its success. Stock options are of two types: incentive stock options (ISOs) and nonqualified stock options (NQSOs).

Incentive stock options can only be used upon shareholder approval. They enjoy a special tax treatment, as the employee realizes no taxable income when receiving the option or exercising it.

The employee is only taxed when the acquired stock is sold, and then the applicable tax rate is the capital-gain tax rate, which is lower than the employee's personal income tax rate. The employee must hold the options and the stock for the required time period. The entrepreneur needs to carefully follow the rules governing incentive stock options, and employees need to observe the rules regarding their exercise.

Nonqualified stock options are different in that there are no restrictions on option price, term, number of options granted or vested in a given year, or the disposition of the stock acquired through exercising an option. There are three different categories of nonqualified stock options. Market value options have an exercise price equal to the fair market value of the company's stock on the date of issuing the option. Discounted stock options have an exercise price below the fair market value of the company's stock on the issuance of the options. Finally, premium-priced options have an exercise price above the fair market value of the company's stock at the date of the issuance. On any nonqualified stock option the employee has tax consequences when exercising the option, not when the option is granted. The employee is taxed at his or her ordinary income rate or the difference between the exercise price and the fair market value of the stock when the option was received. When exercised, the company is entitled to a taxed deduction on the amount of tax to the employee. All things being equal from the company's standpoint, nonqualified stock option plans are preferred over incentive stock option plans.

Restricted Stock

An entrepreneur also can award key employees additional shares of restricted stock—stock not vested until the employee achieves his or her performance objectives or completes a prescribed number of years of employment. The employee is taxed on the value of these shares when they are no longer restricted (are freely transferable) or subject to a substantial use of forfeiture. The company has a tax deduction equal to the amount of income the employee recognized as a tax liability.

Regardless of the controversy and the fact that many stock plans, mainly options, are underwater (having no value with the option price being higher than the present stock price), stock-based compensation is still a good idea for entrepreneurs to use in attracting and retaining key employees, even if stock options are required to be charged against earnings when issued. Companies such as Nanoventions, a micro-optics manufacturer, continue to use them, believing that employees of the company still like them, particularly those that really believe in the product and its future potential.

HIRING PROCESS

Besides having the correct compensation package developed that supports the strategic direction of the company, the entrepreneur needs to establish a process for recruiting the best possible candidates. This process is composed of four basic steps: finding candidates, interviewing, forms for hiring, and developing an employee handbook.

Finding Candidates

One of the keys of the entrepreneur in attracting the right people is finding the right candidates. The best way, of course, is through word of mouth—using your network of entrepreneurs, venture capitalists, bankers, suppliers, and customers to identify some good candidates. Going to industry meetings and trade shows should turn up some names. Contacting professors or previous classmates also should produce some results. If word of mouth fails, then advertisements in appropriate trade journals or newspapers should be employed.

The Interview

In order to hire the right person the entrepreneur needs to have already determined the type of person and skills needed to develop his or her business. Usually this negates hiring someone just like oneself, as individual strengths should complement any weaknesses. Before the interview, the entrepreneur must develop some thoughtful questions while staying within all legal limits. From the legality side, this means staying away from topics such as religion, ethnicity, age, sexual orientation, marital status, or family orientation. Some questions might cover such topics as showing how they would do something, showing how they would respond to real-life challenges posed, soliciting their concept of an ideal position, and obtaining their reaction to the job description of the position you are seeking to fulfill. Throughout the interview the entrepreneur needs to be honest and share his vision of the job and the company.

Forms

The entrepreneur must make sure he or she has all the necessary forms and does all the needed paperwork that goes along with hiring individuals. Since this is usually a tedious, overwhelming task, it is often better for the entrepreneur to get some help. The entrepreneur may want to eliminate the work of payroll, health benefits, and payroll taxes by using a service such as Automatic Data Processing (ADP) or Paycheck. However, only reputable services should be considered for this type of outsourcing. The entrepreneur needs to remember, with or without a service, forms such as W2s, payroll taxes, Social Security, 401Ks, and insurance benefits need to be dealt with and executed on a timely basis.

Employee Handbook

After about the third or fourth employee is hired, the entrepreneur should develop an employee handbook. Often this is best delegated to your first or second employee hired, as they are intimately familiar with the company and what future employees need to know. Having the employee write the handbook will ensure that the relevant questions will be addressed, making the manual a useful tool.

By finding good employees, making their jobs interesting, providing and implementing clear performance standards, providing timely feedback, and rewarding employees' performance in the best possible way, the entrepreneur can attract and retain key employees.

5

Choosing the Right Partner

PROFILE—MARIA RAMOS-STEWART AND JEFF STEWART

Maria Ramos-Stewart started her website development company, Web/Now, in 1998 after losing her marketing position at a large company. This company, based on her hobby, was located in Nashville, Tennessee, where she lived with her husband. The company was so successful in developing websites that it inspired Maria's husband, Jeff, to leave his position of selling computers at a small shop and started his own computer-sales company several years later. Jeff Stewart's business was also doing well when Maria Ramos-Stewart became pregnant and soon after was ordered to bed rest. This made running two successful separate businesses very difficult. Which business should be the focus of the couple's limited time? Should one business be sold? Should an outside partner be obtained?

These were the questions facing Maria and Jeff. Both had very opposite personalities. While Maria was very lively, Jeff was very brusque. Could they be compatible enough to merge their two businesses into one? The nervousness over this decision was perhaps worse for the two of them than the jitters regarding marriage 5 years earlier. Maria and Jeff eventually decided to become business partners and merge their two companies into a new company—TechnoComplete.

Running the new company from their suburban home in Nashville has not always been easy, but the two different management styles and personalities have balanced each other and made it easier to establish the defined role for each in the new company. Because of his experience in selling hardware and software components as a salesperson for a retail computer giant such as CompUSA, Jeff Stewart is responsible for the marketing and sales of TechnoComplete. Based on her previous experience, Maria Ramos-Stewart is in charge of operations of the company, including hiring and firing and maintaining and upgrading the company's computer system.

The new company is a partnership—51 percent owned by Maria and 49 percent by Jeff. Maria is president and chief executive officer. This allows the company, as a double minority-owned business, to have an edge when bidding on certain government contracts. About 18 months after the merger, TechnoComplete won a 5-year contract from the General Service Administration to sell a range of products, including computers, printers, and toners, to government departments. In addition, Maria has developed an Internet site for the company (www.technocomplete.com) enabling customers to buy the company's products online. The new company under the partnership continues to grow, with sales reaching about $800,000 in 2001 and over $1 million in 2002, during a time when many computer retailers were having a significant decrease in business. And, the company recently launched a weekly online magazine for existing and potential customers.

While this is just one form of partnership—a merger, and a unique one at that, involving a married couple owning two different businesses—this next decade will be an era of partnerships of all types. This chapter discusses several "partnership" methods for growth—strategic alliances, joint ventures, mergers, acquisitions, franchising, and licensing—and closes with a discussion of one of the most important aspects of implementing one of these methods—choosing the right partner.

STRATEGIC ALLIANCES

Strategic alliances or strategic combinations offer good opportunities for entrepreneurs to externally grow their ventures. These can range from contractual R&D arrangements to outright acquisitions. Basically, a strategic alliance is an agreement between two or more firms to share the costs, risks, and benefits of developing a business opportunity or coping with a restraint. A good strategic alliance relies on information exchange, joint activities, joint problem solving and decision making, and a balance of power resulting in some shared benefits and burdens. An entrepreneur can have an alliance with a competitor, supplier, customer, government entity, or university.

A strategic alliance is a hybrid organization which, when formed, has an immediate presence and size. Its performance expectations are immediate and externally imposed, with the firms forming the alliance often lacking a common domain or experience base. Alliances frequently cross national and industrial boundaries. An entrepreneur can use an alliance to pool capital and share risk; gain economies of scale; and access new markets, new technologies, and new skills.

The strategic alliances that tend to last and be beneficial for all the partners involved tend to have several characteristics—understanding, excellence and strong contributions, secure sense of priority and finality, and openness and honesty. Understanding means that each firm in the alliance knows that not only do they need each other but each has identified complementary skills sets and assets in each of the other firms in the potential alliance. Excellence and contribution means that each party comes to the alliance with strengths and will add any resources necessary to make the relationship a successful one. No firm should want to use the alliance to compensate for its own shortcomings. When priority and finality are characteristics of the strategic alliance all parties view the alliance as an important part of their business strategy and plan to be a part of the alliance for a long period of time. This leads to the alliance having both a formal legal status and a personal commitment. The final characteristics, openness and honesty, indicate that alliance members freely exchange information and communicate regularly and soon learn to trust each other and want to help other members of the alliance.

There are several issues the entrepreneur should consider before forming a strategic alliance. First, is the alliance the best way to achieve the objectives desired? Is an alliance even feasible? The entrepreneur should make sure the motivations for the strategic alliance are good ones and the advantages of a strategic alliance far outweigh the disadvantages in terms of other options. Second, the entrepreneur needs to consider what form the alliance should take. It is particularly important for the strategic alliance to be structured correctly and have the right governance structure. Third, and perhaps most important, the right partner(s) needs to be selected. Since this is the focus of the last section of this chapter, suffice it to say here that having the right partner will ultimately determine whether the strategic alliance will accomplish its objectives. While coming up with the right strategic partner is as much an art as a science, the entrepreneur should do everything possible to ensure that the best partner possible is selected. Finally, the entrepreneur should make sure that all factors and characteristics previously discussed are in place—to ensure the survival and success of the alliance. Sustaining the mutual cooperation of alliance partners over a period of time will ensure that the alliance provides the maximum benefits to all involved.

JOINT VENTURES

With the increase in business risks, hypercompetition, and failures, joint ventures have occurred with increased regularity and often involve a wide variety of players. A joint venture is not a new concept, but rather has been used as a means of expansion by entrepreneurial firms for a long time.

What is a joint venture? A joint venture is a separate entity that involves a partnership between two or more active partners. Sometimes called *strategic alliances*, joint ventures can involve a wide variety of partners that include universities, not-for-profit organizations, businesses, and the public sector. Joint ventures have occurred between such rivals as General Motors and Toyota, and General Electric and Westinghouse. Joint ventures have occurred between U.S. and foreign concerns in order to penetrate and perform in a global market. These global alliances have been a good conduit by which an entrepreneur can enter an international market.

Although there are many different types of joint venture arrangements, the most common is still between two or more companies. For example, Boeing/Mitsubishi/Fuji/Kawasaki entered into a joint venture for the production of small aircraft in order to share technology and cut costs. To cut costs, agreements were made between Ford and Mesasurex in the area of factory automation, and General Motors and Toyota in the area of automobile production. Other joint ventures have had different objectives, such as entering new markets (Corning and Ciba-Geigy and Kodak and Cetus), entering foreign markets (AT&T and Olivetti), and raising capital and expanding markets (U.S. Steel and Phong Iron and Steel).

Industry-university agreements created for the purpose of doing research are another type of joint venture agreement that has seen increasing use. However, some major problems have kept this type of joint venture from proliferating even faster. A profit corporation has the objective of obtaining tangible results, such as a patent, from its research investment and wants all proprietary rights. Universities want to share in the possible financial returns from the patent, but the university agreements want to make the knowledge available through research papers. In spite of these problems, numerous industry-university teams have been established. In one joint venture agreement in robotics, for example, Westinghouse retains patent rights while Carnegie-Mellon receives a percentage of any license royalties. The university also has the right to publish the research results as long as it withholds from publication any critical information that might adversely affect the patent.

MERGERS AND ACQUISITIONS

Another way the entrepreneur can expand the venture is by merging or acquiring an existing business. Acquisitions provide an excellent means of expanding a business by entering new markets or new product areas. One entrepreneur acquired a chemical manufacturing company after becoming familiar with its problems and operations as a company supplier. An acquisition is the purchase of an entire company, or part of a company; the company is completely absorbed and no longer exists independently. An acquisition can take many forms, depending on the goals and position of the parties involved in the transaction, the amount of money involved, and the type of company.

Although one of the key issues in buying a business is agreeing on a price, successful acquisition of a business actually involves much, much more. In fact, often the structure of the deal can be more important to the resultant success of the transaction than the actual price. One radio station was successful after being acquired by a company primarily because the previous owner loaned the money and took no principal payment (only interest) on the loan until the third year of operation.

From a strategic viewpoint, a prime concern of the entrepreneurial firm is maintaining the focus of the new venture as a whole. Whether the acquisition will become the core of the new business or rather represents a needed capability—such as a distribution outlet, sales force, or production facility—the entrepreneur must ensure that it fits into the overall direction and structure of the strategic plan of the present venture.

There are many advantages in acquiring an existing business for an entrepreneur. The most significant advantage in acquiring an existing business is that the acquired firm has an established image and track record. Also, in the case of acquiring an existing business, there is no question concerning the new customers since they are already familiar with the location. A third advantage is that the entrepreneur acquires an established marketing structure with known suppliers, wholesalers, retailers, and/or manufacturers' reps. Another advantage is the fact that the actual cost of acquiring a business can be lower than other methods of expansion. Additionally, the employees of an existing business can be an important asset to the acquisition process.

Finally, since the entrepreneur does not have to be concerned with finding suppliers and channel members, hiring new employees, or creating customer awareness, more time can be spent assessing opportunities to expand or strengthen the existing business.

Although there are many advantages in acquiring an existing business, there are also disadvantages. Most ventures that are for sale have an erratic, marginally successful, or even unprofitable track record.

Second, sometimes an entrepreneur is overconfident and assumes that he or she can succeed where others have failed. Third, often when a business changes hands, key employees also leave. Key employee loss can be devastating to an entrepreneur who is acquiring a business since the value of the business is often a reflection of the efforts of the employees. Finally, it is possible that the actual purchase price is inflated due to the established image, customer base, channel members, or suppliers.

While valuation is the focus of Chapter 13, some of the key factors used in determining price are: earnings (past and potential), assets, owner's equity, stock value, customer base, strength of the distribution network, personnel, and image. When these factors are difficult to value, the entrepreneur may want to get outside help. The price paid should provide the opportunity to get a reasonable payback and good return on the investment.

There are three widely used valuation approaches—asset, cash flow, and earnings—that the entrepreneur can use to determine a fair price (or value) of an acquisition. Some helpful, important factors in the evaluation process that measure profitability, activity, and liquidity are indicated in Table 5-1.

A merger—or a transaction involving two or possibly more companies in which only one company survives—is another method of expanding a venture. Acquisitions are so similar to mergers that at times the two terms are used interchangeably. A key concern in any merger (or acquisition) is the legality of the purchase. The Department of Justice frequently issues guidelines for horizontal, vertical, and conglomerate mergers, which further define the interpretation

Table 5-1. Key negative factors in evaluating a firm.

- One-person management
- Poor corporate communications
- Few management tools being used
- Insufficient financial controls
- Highly leveraged, thinly capitalized
- Variations and poorly prepared financial statements
- Sales growth with no increase in bottom line
- Dated and poorly managed inventory
- Aging accounts receivable
- No change in products or customers

that will be made in enforcing the Sherman Act and Clayton Act. Since the guidelines are extensive and technical, the entrepreneur should secure adequate legal advice when any issues arise.

FRANCHISING

Franchising also represents an opportunity for an entrepreneur to expand his or her business. In the context of franchising, the entrepreneur will be trained and supported in the marketing by the franchisor and will be using a name that has an established image. Franchising is also an alternative means by which an entrepreneur may expand his or her business by having others pay for the use of the name, process, product, and/or service. In January 1980, Jim Fowler decided to franchise his housecleaning venture, Merry Maids. The concept of a housecleaning service provided on a weekly or biweekly basis was difficult for the public to understand. Through franchising, the venture achieved more credibility, which in turn helped facilitate franchise sales. Now operating in 48 states and in a number of foreign countries, Merry Maids has grown to be a significant business. Fowler's attention to image, which included required, standardized employee uniforms, quality training for franchisees, and the use of a line of pretested cleaning products, has allowed him to impressively expand a housecleaning business and to offer opportunities for entrepreneurs to become successful businesspeople.

Franchising may be defined as an arrangement whereby the manufacturer or sole distributor of a trademarked product or service gives exclusive rights of local distribution to independent retailers in return for their payment of royalties and conformance to standardized operating procedures. The person offering the franchise is known as the franchisor. The franchisee is the person who purchases the franchise and is given the opportunity to enter a new business with a better chance to succeed than if he or she were to start a new business from scratch.

Advantages of Franchising

The advantages a franchisor gains through franchising are related to expansion risk, capital requirements, and cost advantages that result from extensive buying power. For example, Fred DeLuca would not have been able to achieve the size and scope of Subway without franchising it. In order to use franchising as an expansion method, the franchisor must have established value and credibility that someone else is willing to buy.

Expansion Risk

The most obvious advantage of franchising for an entrepreneur is that it allows the venture to expand quickly using little capital. This advantage is significant when we reflect on the problems and issues that an entrepreneur faces in trying to manage and grow a new venture. A franchisor can expand a business nationally and even internationally by authorizing and selling franchises in selected locations. The capital necessary for this expansion is much less than it would be without franchising. Just think of the capital needed by DeLuca to build over 8000 Subway sandwich shops.

Cost Advantages

The mere size of a franchised company offers many advantages to the franchisees. The franchisor can purchase supplies in large quantities, thus achieving economies of scale that would not have been possible otherwise. Many franchise businesses produce parts, accessories, packaging, and raw materials in large quantities, then, in turn, sell these to the franchisees. Franchisees are often required to purchase these items as part of the franchise agreement, and they usually benefit from lower prices.

One of the biggest cost advantages of franchising a business is the ability to commit larger sums of money to advertising. Each franchisee contributes a percentage of sales (usually 1 to 2 percent) to an advertising pool. This pooling of resources allows the franchisor to conduct advertising in major media across a wide geographic area. If the business had not been franchised, the company would have had to provide funds for the entire advertising budget.

Disadvantages of Franchising

Franchising is not always the best option for an entrepreneur. Anyone investing in a franchise should investigate the opportunity thoroughly. Problems between the franchisor and franchisee are common and have recently begun to receive more attention from the government and trade associations.

The disadvantages to the franchisee usually center on the inability of the franchisor to provide services, advertising, and location. When promises made in the franchise agreement are not kept, the franchisee may be left without any support in important areas. For example, Curtis Bean bought a dozen franchises in Checkers of America Inc., a firm that provides auto inspection services. After losing $200,000, Bean and other franchisees filed a lawsuit claiming that the franchisor had misrepresented advertising costs and had made false claims, including one that no experience was necessary to own a franchise.

The franchisee may also face the problem of a franchisor failing or being bought out by another company. No one knows this better than Vincent Niagra, an owner of three Window Works franchises. Niagra had invested about $1 million in these franchises when the franchise was sold in 1988 to Apogee Enterprises and then resold in 1992 to a group of investors. This caused many franchises to fail, leaving a total of 50 franchises. The failure of these franchises has made it difficult for Niagra to continue because customers are apprehensive about doing business with him for fear that he will go out of business. No support services that had been promised were available.

Types of Franchises

There are three available types of franchises. The first type is the dealership, a form commonly found in the automobile industry. Here, manufacturers use franchises to distribute their product lines. These dealerships act as the retail stores for the manufacturer. In some instances, they are required to meet quotas established by the manufacturers, but as is the case for any franchise, they benefit from the advertising and management support provided by the franchisor.

The most common type of franchise is the type that offers a name, image, and method of doing business, such as McDonald's, Subway, KFC, Midas, Dunkin' Donuts, and Holiday Inn. There are many of these types of franchises, and their listings, with information, can be found in various sources.

A third type of franchise offers services. These include personnel agencies, income tax preparation companies, and realtors. These franchises have established names and reputations and methods of doing business. In some instances, such as real estate, the franchisee has actually been operating a business and then applies to become a member of the franchise.

LICENSING

Another method of externally growing an entrepreneurial venture is through licensing. As was the case with franchising, licensing provides the entrepreneur a vehicle for growing the venture and obtaining positive cash flow while avoiding dilution of ownership or an increase in debt. When using a licensing agreement, an entrepreneur grants the licensee the right to manufacture its product, sell its services, and/or use any intellectual property such as its patent, technology, or trademark. For this right(s), the licensee pays the entrepreneur a fixed

Table 5-2. Favorable circumstances for licensing.

- Company lacks capital, managerial resources, knowledge, or commitment to a foreign market.
- Company wants to test viability of a market.
- Technology is not central to company's core business.
- Strong possibility of acquiring new technology.
- Market too small to warrant any other activity.
- Laws of country restrict other options.
- Risk of nationalization in country too great.
- Licensee could become a future competitor.
- Rapid rate of technological change.

payment, and/or a regular royalty sum usually based on a per-unit or percent-of-sales basis. The licensee can only use the rights in a defined geographical area and for the designated purposes.

There are several circumstances that make licensing a very viable alternative (see Table 5-2). These include lacking capital or other managerial resources; wanting to test the viability of a market; feeling that a technology is not central to a company's core business or that new, improved technology can be acquired; feeling that a market is too small to warrant full activity; reducing the possibility of the licensee becoming a future competitor; restrictive country laws or nationalization risk high; and/or the technology is changing at such a rapid rate that the licensed technology will soon be obsolete. For example, the McGraw-Hill Companies gave the author a license to publish his best-selling book *Entrepreneurship* in the Slovene language without the company's fee because the potential market was too small to warrant the costs of producing the Slovenian edition. The total population of Slovenia is only about 1.5 million people.

PARTNER SELECTION

By far the most important thing to ensure that a strategic alliance, a merger or acquisition, or a franchising or licensing arrangement is successful is to select the right partner. In fact, choosing the right partner in any business dealing is key. Partnering with the right manufacturer's representative or other member of the distribution channel is equally crucial for the successful sales and distribution of the company's products.

Partner Selecting Procedure

An entrepreneur should establish a solid procedure for partner selection. First, as many promising candidates as possible should be identified. All possible sources should be exhausted such as trade listings, trade associations, and other industry information sources. Personal contracts with other entrepreneurs should be used as well as attendance at appropriate trade shows. Second, once the list has been obtained, specific screening criteria should be established that are appropriate for the entrepreneur's objective in partner selecting. These should include size parameters, product and/or service requirements, and market capabilities. Third, as much information as possible should be collected on each potential partner. This information can be in published form such as company reports or pamphlets, articles in trade journals, Better Business Bureau reports, or other U.S. government reports. Also, data should be collected directly from informed third parties such as customers, firms doing business with the potential partner, and other knowledgeable individuals or companies. Fourth, an initial meeting with the several (usually three to four) potential partners selected should occur. An initial agreement of possible terms should be discussed and any present or future issues that may affect the partnership identified and resolved. References should be obtained and subsequently checked and each reference should be asked for other references. Fifth, based on this analysis, one potential partner should be identified and time should be taken to get to know the prospect as well as possible before making the commitment. Meals should be shared and a complete understanding developed. Finally, once a good feeling and procedure for a working relationship has been established, a formal legal agreement should be executed and the partnership begun.

Sometimes potential partners are those who are thought of the least. For example, if an entrepreneur needs a technology partner, perhaps the National Aeronautical Space Agency (NASA) may be a good fit. In some cases, NASA scientists actually become true partners and show the entrepreneurial company how to make a better product at a lower cost and sometimes even help find customers. The NASA relationship was a beneficial one for ADMA Products, Inc. The company, located in Twinsburg, Ohio, manufactured powder metallurgy products and was interested in a NASA-developed composite material that could be used as a lubricant in high-temperature applications. Through one of NASA's six regional centers—the Great Lakes Industrial Technology Center—ADMA Products, Inc. created a commercialization plan and now licenses the technology to produce metallurgical powder and parts for mechanical devices. The company is continuing to work with NASA to develop further applications for the technology.

Characteristics of a Good Partner

A good partner, like NASA for ADMA Products, Inc., has several characteristics. First, a good partner helps the entrepreneur achieve his or her strategic goals, whether these goals are acquiring a new technology, accessing a new market(s), reducing costs, or obtaining other needed competencies. Second, a good partner shares the entrepreneur's vision of the purpose and outcomes of the partnership. There should never be any differences in the expectations of how the partnership should operate and what the results should be. Finally, a good partner would never exploit the partnership for his or her own gain. Each partner is open and honest and deals ethically with the other.

Assessment Criteria for Choosing a Partner

In order to effectively pick a compatible partner, an entrepreneur should establish specific criteria that are important in partner selection. While these need to be company specific, at least three criteria should be considered. First, the partner company needs to be internally interrelated and networked. Hierarchical, "silo" management should not be present, as this would lead to difficulties in the partnership without significant restructuring to cross-functionalize the entire partner company. Second, the partner company should have a good communication network and be willing to establish solid communication protocols with the entrepreneur. A good partnership depends on timely communications, both internally and externally. Today this often takes the form of good electronic communication. The email system established should make sure to specify who tells what to whom and when, and make sure no one is left out of the loop. Finally, the partner company should have a strong, loyal customer base. These customers should be regularly communicated with and leveraged to the extent possible. When a good partner is chosen the entrepreneur has the opportunity to further grow his or her venture through some outside mechanism.

6

Being Flexible and Creative

PROFILE—DENVER HOPKINS

Denver Hopkins was born in 1967. His father was a preacher, and he grew up loving to explore caves, something he continued to do as a holiday during his various jobs. His job as a technology strategist at Compaq Computer in Houston, Texas, focused on developing 5-year technology plans for the company, which would then need funding and implementation. This involved attending conferences and reading journals, to be in a position to present the technology future for the various divisions of the company.

Although he really liked his job, Denver left Compaq in 1996 to start Thought Farm, a technology consulting company. The company made money immediately and began to grow rapidly, doubling its revenues each year for the first 2 years. Thought Farm developed and sometimes implemented technology plans for various companies, including developing and launching e-commerce sites.

Denver Hopkins used the money from his 401K at Compaq to start the company, but he soon found that he needed more capital to grow the venture. Instead of getting some equity infusion, he borrowed money to expand the business, personally guaranteeing each bank loan. Payroll increased significantly along with the size of the debt. In one 4-month period in 1998 payroll tripled. The increased pressures to continue to grow the business and meet all the financial obligations and burdens of the company significantly affected Denver Hopkins. Being so deeply in debt from both a business and personal perspective, he went from being a risk taker to being so risk-averse that his goal became to never make a mistake.

In 1999, Thought Farm stopped making money, and Denver Hopkins felt he could never leave the office. He often gave up sleep in order to fulfill his love of exploring and mapping caves in his free time. His behavior continued to change and he often spent hours trying to fix the many company problems. Between 1999 and 2002 Thought Farm continued to go downhill and was slowly dying. Since his company was an open-book company, employees could see the gradual demise, and some stayed without pay to try to help, due to their devotion to Denver. He continued to cut staff and asked all the employees to leave and find themselves a better job; still two refused.

In the fall of 2001, Thought Farm had two employees in addition to Denver Hopkins and a few projects—a small company very similar to the initial successful start-up company. Denver Hopkins realized this was what he really liked, so he broke the lease on the building in Houston and went back to working on what he loved best—developing visionary technology plans for clients by reading and attending conferences. Would Thought Farm have been able to grow had professional managers been hired to run the company? Maybe, but it is hard to tell. Today, Denver Hopkins wants to keep his company small but is unsure of what he will do with the company in the future.

Denver Hopkins was fortunate to survive an ordeal that spells disaster for many entrepreneurial companies. He and his company had enough flexibility to change directions and, in his case, downsize to return to the original concept of the company. This chapter addresses the common mistake of not maintaining flexibility by looking at the overall general flexibility of the company and the need for continuous innovation and creativity, continually developing new products that are customer-focused by establishing a sound product planning and development process, and establishing a sound evaluation procedure.

COMPANY FLEXIBILITY

In rapidly changing global markets entrepreneurs who want to be successful and stay competitive must develop some unusual qualities in their companies. They must have their companies become both flexible and stable—flexible in order to respond quickly to competitive threats, environmental changes, and consumer changes and stable in order to learn and grow based on their strategies and competitive advantages.

The flexibility of your company to adapt and respond quickly to change means that you must focus on modification and adaptation. Generally, more flexible companies are thought of as having less top-down control and more team and individual empowerment. The job of the entrepreneur is to make sure that flexibility flows throughout the organization.

Types of Flexibility

There are three types of organizational flexibility: operational flexibility, structural flexibility, and strategic flexibility. Operational flexibility means that the entrepreneur's company has freedom in the routines that are based on the existing structures or goals of the organization. It allows rapid response to changes that are familiar and result in short-term changes in the firm's routine and activity. This can take the form of increasing or decreasing the production output, using temporary help, or building up inventories for a short period of time. Structural flexibility refers to the capability of the entrepreneur and his or her management team to be able to adapt its decision making and communication process within the organization's structure as well as to anticipate how quickly this can be done. In responding to significant change, this may take the form of establishing small production units, altering some control systems, or changing some organizational positions and responsibilities. Strategic flexibility relates to the goals of the entrepreneur's organization. This type of flexibility is needed when the company faces unfamiliar changes that have far-reaching consequences. Because there is no specific experience and no established way to cope with these types of changes, the entrepreneur may have to change his or her current strategies and develop an entirely new game plan. This may result in creating new products, developing new advertising and promotion campaigns, changing the production methods, or engaging in lobbying activities to influence government laws and legislation.

Creating Flexibility Advantages

The ability to respond quickly to any change gives the entrepreneur a number of advantages, which can be leveraged strategically. These can take several different forms that create significant strategic advantages. A company that is able to deliver products and services in the form and level of quality desired in a timely manner has a sustainable competitive advantage. The flexibility to introduce new products, brands, or models that preempt competitive actions and establish a strong market position can help the entrepreneurial company achieve strong first-mover advantages.

Company flexibility can also allow adjustment of supply to particular demand conditions. This response flexibility in adjusting supply volume and product mix reduces costs in low-growth conditions and increases sales in hot, growing markets. The ability to exchange people, machines, operations, and processes leads to significant adaptive advantages.

Finally, the flexibility to produce the right product efficiently and effectively gives the entrepreneurial company tremendous cost advantages. This can be translated into higher value, lower-priced products with good margins being delivered to the marketplace. This means that flexible response from activities such as production and distribution is needed.

CREATIVITY

Having flexibility in the company means that the entrepreneur has fostered a most important element in his or her organizational culture—creativity. The highly centralized, bureaucratic environment of many companies hinders creativity by stressing the consequence of failure; having excessive formalization of policies, procedures, relationships, and rules; and allowing little time (if any) for creative thinking and experimenting.

In a similar fashion, individuals create their own barriers to creativity. These barriers include searching for the one right answer, blindly following the rules and procedures, avoiding ambiguity, fearing looking foolish, fearing mistakes and failures, and believing that they are not creative.

Given the individual and organizational barriers, it is important for the entrepreneur to establish an organizational culture that allows and, in fact, encourages people in the company to engage in the creative process. The steps in the creative process can be followed to solve any problem or goal operating in the company: preparation, investigation, transformation, incubation, illumination, verification, and implementation.

The most difficult aspect of this creative process is preparation. How does an entrepreneur unlock his or her own creativity if needed or, more importantly, the creativity of the company's employees and managers? Methods for doing this are shown in Table 6-1, a few of which will be discussed here.

Checklist Method

One method that is simple to implement is the checklist method, where a new idea is developed through a list of related issues or suggestions. The entrepreneur can use the list of questions or statements to guide the direction of developing entirely new ideas or concentrating on specific "idea" areas. The checklist may take any form and be of any length. One general checklist is: (1) Put to other uses? (2) Adapt? (3) Modify? (4) Magnify? (5) Minimize? (6) Substitute? (7) Rearrange? (8) Reverse? or (9) Combine?

Free Association

One of the simplest yet most effective methods that entrepreneurs can use to generate new ideas is free association. This technique is helpful

Table 6-1. Creativity and creative problem-solving techniques.

- Brainstorming
- Reverse brainstorming
- Synectics
- Gordon method
- Checklist method
- Free association
- Forced relationships
- Collective notebook method
- Heuristics
- Scientific method
- Kepner-Tregoe method
- Value analysis
- Attribute listing method
- Morphological analysis
- Matrix charting
- Sequence-attribute/modification matrix
- Inspired (big-dream) approach
- Parameter analysis

in developing an entirely new slant to a problem. First, a word or phrase related to the problem is written down, then another, and another, with each new word attempting to add something new to the ongoing thought processes, thereby creating a chain of ideas ending with a new product idea emerging.

Forced Relationships

Forced relationships, as the name implies, is the process of forcing relationships among some product combinations. It is a technique that asks questions about objects or ideas in an effort to develop a new idea. The new combination and eventual concept is developed through a five-step process.

1. Isolate the elements of the problem.
2. Find the relationships between these elements.
3. Record the relationships in an orderly form.
4. Analyze the resulting relationships to find ideas or patterns.
5. Develop new ideas from these patterns.

Collective Notebook Method

In the collective notebook method, a small notebook that easily fits in a pocket containing a statement of the problem, blank pages, and any pertinent background data is distributed. Participants consider the problem and its possible solutions, recording ideas at least once, but preferably three times, a day. At the end of a month, a list of the best ideas is developed, along with any suggestions. This technique can also be used with a group of individuals who record their ideas, giving their notebooks to a central coordinator who summarizes all the material. The summary becomes the topic of a final creative focus group discussion by the group participants. Confidentiality must be guaranteed.

INNOVATION

Creativity is the key ingredient ensuring that innovation is constantly occurring in the entrepreneurial company. One thing successful entrepreneurial companies have in common is that their success derives in a large measure from innovation. While indeed competitive advantage can come from size or asset ownership, the largest sustainable competitive advantage comes from the ability to mobilize knowledge, technology, and experience to create new products, processes, and services.

There are three types of innovation: radical, changing, and line extensions. Radical innovations give birth to an entirely new industry. These innovations typically transcend present consumer desires by serving needs that have not yet been articulated. As such, these are the most difficult and costly innovations for the entrepreneur, as they take a great deal of time and information (usually in the form of marketing dollars) to gain acceptance, which results in eventual sales. There are few radical innovations. The airplane, light bulb, telephone, scotch tape, express delivery service, and the use of the Internet are a few examples. These are transforming innovations that radically affect a person's lifestyle upon their adoption.

The second type of innovation is not so radical and changes the basis of competition in an industry. These are usually more widely embraced by customers in a shorter period of time than radical innovations. Post-It Notes, pizza delivery, and microwave ovens would be examples of this type of innovation.

The final type of innovation has the least disruptive effect on consumers and their lifestyles. These are called line extensions and are usually closely aligned with explicit customer needs. As such, they require the least amount of time and less information than the other two types of innovations. Post-It Notes in multiple colors and shapes, various lengths of time of express delivery, and higher-speed Internet access are examples of line extensions.

In order to allow as much innovation as possible, the entrepreneur needs to understand that product innovations (products/services) as well as process innovation (changing the way products/services are created and delivered) can come from a wide variety of sources, both internal and external to the company.

THE PRODUCT PLANNING AND DEVELOPMENT PROCESS

The need for a new source of profits, coupled with the high rate of failure of new products, requires a continuous search for sources of new product ideas, as well as for new product evaluation at all stages in the product planning and development process. Although the product planning development process varies from industry to industry, as well as from firm to firm within a given industry, its activities generally follow the pattern illustrated in Figure 6-1. The process can be divided into five major stages: idea stage, concept stage, product development stage, test marketing stage, and commercialization stage.

In the idea stage, suggestions for new products are obtained from all possible sources, and all available devices for generating new product ideas should be employed. Frequently one of the creative problem-solving techniques previously discussed can be used to develop marketable ideas. Regardless of the source, these ideas should be carefully screened to determine which are good enough to require more detailed

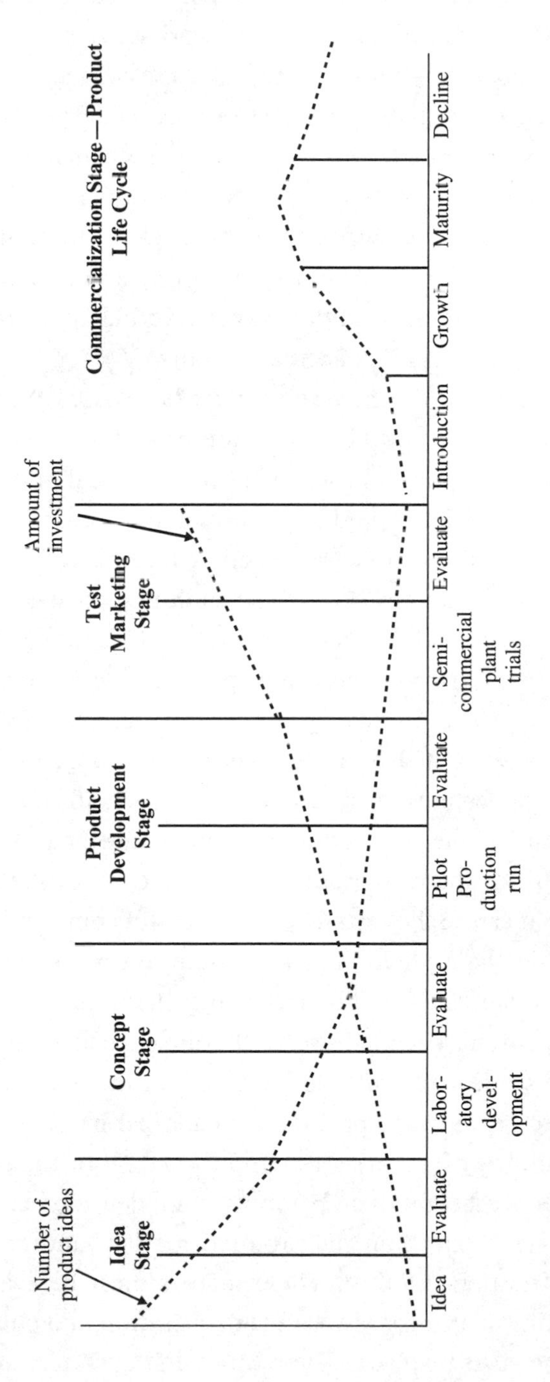

Figure 6-1. The product planning and development process.

investigation. It is important for the company to establish objectives and define growth areas to provide a framework for this analysis.

Ideas passing the initial screening enter the concept stage, where they are developed into more elaborate product concepts. In evaluating the product concept, a company should keep in mind its own strengths and weaknesses, as well as the needs of potential buyers. A tentative business plan consisting of product features and a marketing program should be developed and evaluated by a sample of potential buyers. This presentation can be verbal or pictorial; the latter generally produces more accurate results.

Once the concept for the new product has passed the screening criteria, it is further developed into a prototype and tested. This occurs in the product development stage, where the technical and economic aspects of the potential new product are explored, sometimes by assigning specific areas needed in the development to members of research and development. Unless excessive capital expenditures make it impossible, laboratory products should be created for testing. Once a more complete design is achieved, these products can be produced on a pilot-run basis, which allows for some production control and product testing. The products can be evaluated by in-use consumer testing, to determine whether they have features superior to products currently available.

The results of the product development stage help develop the marketing plan for the new product. In some cases a market test is undertaken to increase the certainty of successful commercialization. This last step in the evaluation process—the test marketing stage—can provide actual sales results, indicating the acceptance level of consumers in real-market conditions. Of course, positive results, cannot guarantee success, but they do indicate that the new product has the potential to be marketed profitably on a larger basis.

The feasibility of a market test and the extent of the evaluation in each stage of the product planning and development process depend to a great extent on the product, market, and competitive situation confronting the firm. These factors must be evaluated in terms of the time elapsing between idea generation and commercialization and the costs involved. These times and costs should then be compared with the high costs of unsuccessful commercialization. Even though great technological advances have occurred and the new products have been developed, they are not immediately marketable. The average time elapsing between conception and new product realization is about 10 to 15 years; for example, it took 6 years for the video tape recorder and 32 years for the heart pacemaker. It does not appear that this time period is becoming any shorter; a matter of concern to the government, business, and academic sectors.

The long time period in the product planning and development process also must be carefully weighed against the cost of the evaluation process and the costs of commercialization. Even though they eliminate 90 percent of the available ideas, the idea and concept stages should still take very little time and money—only about 10 percent of the total time and expenditures involved in the entire product planning and development process. The product development stage should use about 30 percent of the total expenditures and 40 percent of the total time, and the test marketing stage should take about 12 percent of the total money and 20 percent of the time. In the commercialization stage, about 50 percent of the total expenditures occur in only 23 percent of the total time. Given these time and cost allocations, a company needs to actively develop sources for new product ideas so that the product planning and development process can continually result in the commercialization of successful new products.

SOURCES OF NEW PRODUCT IDEAS

There are many sources of new product ideas. These include customers, the competition, distribution channels, the federal government, research and development, the company sales force, upper-level management, and employee suggestions.

METHODS OF GENERATING IDEAS

Even with a wide variety of sources available, coming up with an idea can still be a difficult task. The entrepreneur can use several methods to help generate and test new ideas, including reverse brainstorming and attributed listing.

Reverse Brainstorming

The reverse brainstorming approach is a modification of brainstorming, listing the weaknesses of a particular product. This list of negative attributes then provides the direction for discussion on new products and product improvements. The general advantages and disadvantages of this approach are similar to those of the brainstorming technique. One additional limitation is that the approach focuses on the perceived problems of a product. These may not be important problems for all consumers.

Attribute Listing

The attribute listing technique involves listing the existing attributes of a product idea or area and then modifying them until a new combination of attributes emerges that will improve the product idea or area. A small company manufacturing pallets used for shipping or moving a product on a conveyor along an assembly line wanted to devise a better product. It listed the attributes that defined the existing pallets, such as wood composition, rectangular runners, and accessibility from two sides by a forklift, and then examined each attribute for any possible change that would improve the product. For example, the wood composition could be changed to plastic, resulting in a cheaper price. The rectangular wooden runners could be replaced by cups, making the pallets easier to store and allowing them to be accessed from all four sides for easier pick-up. Through attribute listing, this small company achieved an idea for a much-improved product that was successfully commercialized.

One major drawback to attribute listing is that it focuses on the product at hand and therefore cannot be used in all new product situations, particularly when no existing product is yet available. The technique may even stifle imaginative thinking to some extent. Yet, as in the case of the pallet manufacturer, attribute listing is often a useful method for developing new and/or improved product ideas.

EVALUATING NEW IDEAS

At each stage of the product planning and development process, criteria for evaluation need to be established. These criteria should be broad, yet quantitative enough to screen the product carefully in the particular stage of development. Criteria should be developed to evaluate the new product in terms of market opportunity, competition, the marketing system, financial factors, and production factors.

A market opportunity in the form of a new or current need for the product idea must exist. The determination of market demand is by far the most important criterion of a proposed new product idea. Assessment of the market opportunity and size needs to include consideration of the following: the characteristics and attitudes of consumers or industries that may buy the product, the size of this potential market in dollars and units, the nature of the market with respect to its stage in the life cycle (growing or declining), and the share of the market the product could reasonably capture.

Current competing producers, prices, and marketing policies also should be evaluated, particularly in terms of their impact on the market share of the proposed product. The new product should be able to compete successfully with products already on the market by having features that will meet or overcome current and anticipated competition. The new product should have some unique differential advantage based on an evaluation of all competitive products filling the same consumer needs.

The new product should be compatible with existing management capabilities and marketing strategies. The firm should be able to use its marketing experience and other expertise in this new product effort. For example, General Electric would have a far less difficult time adding a new kitchen appliance to its line than Procter & Gamble. Several factors should be considered in evaluating the degree of fit: the degree to which the ability and time of the present sales force can be transferred to the new product, the ability to sell the new product through the company's established channels of distribution, and the ability to "piggy-back" the advertising and promotion required to introduce the new product.

The proposed product should be able to be supported by and contribute to the company's financial structure. This should be evaluated by estimating manufacturing cost per unit, sales and advertising expense per unit, and amount of capital and inventory required. The break-even point and the long-term profit outlook for the product need to be determined.

Along with financial criteria, the compatibility of the new product's production requirements with existing plant, machinery, and personnel should be determined. If the new product idea cannot be integrated into existing manufacturing processes, not only is the new idea less positive, but new plant and production costs as well as amount of plant space must be determined if the new product is to be manufactured efficiently. All required materials needed in the production of the product should be available and accessible in sufficient quantity.

CREATIVITY METRICS

But how do you know if you are really using the creativity of your organization and having regular product and process innovations and successful new products and services? Each entrepreneur needs to establish sensible metrics for his or her company in this area. Some indicators used by other entrepreneurial companies include sales of new products as a percent of total company sales, number of patents, number of technology platforms, amount spent on research and development, amount of time set aside for thinking about things not directly related to the specific job, and any awards received for creative/innovative accomplishments. The standards established should take into account the nature of the industry and the market.

Some companies are way off the curve. Invacare, a leader in home health-care products, has the goal of having 90 percent of its revenue stream from new products introduced over the last 24-month period and increasing its investment in research and development from 1.7 percent of sales to 3 percent of sales over the next 5 years, for a total expenditure of approximately $170 million. According to

A. Malachi Mixon III, chairman and CEO, "You have to continually focus on delivering new quality products to your customers." Regardless of the metrics established, an entrepreneur needs to avoid the big mistake of not delivering new, quality products and make sure his or her company is flexible, creative, and innovative with new products and services constantly being introduced to the market.

7

Building a Strong Company

PROFILE—TRUETT CATHY

In 1967 Truett Cathy started his company, Chick-fil-A, a fast-food chicken restaurant, now a chain, juggling profit and prayer. This private, family-owned business has used these principles to become the number two fast-food chicken chain in the world in 2002, with over 1055 restaurants and revenues of over $1.2 billion. The fast-food chain is closed on Sundays and spends millions each year on college scholarships, foster homes, and summer camps. *QSR Magazine* recently ranked its drive-through service as number one in the industry. Except for a few hundred licensed stores in airports and on college campuses, the company owns most of its restaurants, each of which is run by a manager who shares in the profits but not the ownership of the company. Typically, when the company is expanding to a new location, the selected manager puts up between $5000 and $10,000 and is guaranteed a minimum income. Each manager pays the company 15 percent of the gross revenue and 50 percent of the profits of his or her particular restaurant(s). The company has grown by carefully selecting capable, hungry entrepreneurs for each of its stores. The company prefers this private family ownership rather than franchising or being a publicly traded company. Managers of large stand-alone Chick-fil-A restaurants can earn upward of $140,000 a year.

The company, now under Truett's son, Dan, has some aggressive growth plans. Chick-fil-A will add about 80 stores in 2003, mostly in the Southeast, and plans to add an additional 420 stores by 2006. Plans are also in the works for adding such new menu items as fresh-squeezed lemonade smoothies and a spicey salad. Prayer is welcome at the company's headquarters or stores, as Chick-fil-A's religious base and inspiration has served the company well, especially during these times of corporate scandals.

What a contrast there is between Truett and Dan Cathy of Chick-fil-A and Dennis Kozlowski, the former CEO of Tyco. Dennis allegedly has taken over $600 million from Tyco through theft, misuse of loans, and selling shares of company stock while concealing what was really happening. While honing a reputation for frugality and stating that he did not believe in perks, Dennis Kozlowski allegedly siphoned millions from Tyco to buy yachts, paintings, and luxury apartments. His $30 million Fifth Avenue apartment supposedly has a $6000 shower curtain and a $15,000 poodle-shaped umbrella stand. Perhaps his greatest exploitation was having Tyco pay for half of the $2.1 million birthday party of his wife, Karen. This price tag included flying 75 people to the Italian island of Sardinia and showcasing a big ice sculpture of David at the party.

This chapter explores avoiding the mistake of either going belly-up (failing) or having the company fall far short of its potential by looking at various aspects of building a strong company. Maintaining core values, building strong brands, developing competence, insisting on ethical behavior, having a good leadership style, and implementing sound succession planning will provide the foundation for a long, healthy life for your company.

MAINTAINING CORE VALUES

In an era of hypercompetition and economic turbulence amid skepticism about the value and integrity of businesses, it is most important for the entrepreneur to have a well-articulated company mission and a consistently practiced set of core values. As was discussed in Chapter 3, employees today more than ever before, are seeking meaning in their jobs and want their work to be purposeful. While compensation is important, as was discussed in Chapter 4, the real motivation of most employees goes far beyond monetary reward; a higher-order motivation arises out of believing that your work has a purpose and is a part of something larger in the company context that will achieve something truly worthwhile. The mission of the company that delivers a clear sense of direction and purpose is the best way to constantly give value and meaning to your employees. Table 7-1 presents the central concepts distilled from the mission statements of such selected U.S. companies as 3M, General Electric, Marriott, and Wal-Mart. When analyzing these mission statements, several underlying themes emerge. First, successful strong companies feel that their most valuable asset is their people and will go to great lengths to make sure it is fun to go to work. Given enough time and resources, any innovative product or service can be replicated and often even bettered. However, it is extremely hard to replicate, even in the long run, a company with highly motivated, loyal employees who are having fun.

Second, successful, strong companies focus on customer satisfaction. The purpose of any company is serving its customers. Superior service and satisfied customers produce greater market share and the ability to sustain profitable margins, which leads to a greater growth rate and profitability, which maximizes shareholder wealth. A company's ability to survive and prosper is directly related to how well it serves its customers, the focus of Chapter 8.

Third, successful companies continually innovate, constantly improving not only the quality of their own products and services but also the quality of life of their stakeholders. This focus on creativity and continuous innovation ensures that the company is always at the cutting edge of technology, producing high-quality, reliable products and services, the focus of Chapter 6. Finally, successful companies operate with honesty and integrity. The scandals of today at Tyco, Worldcom, Enron, and Adelphia show the importance of this aspect of a good mission statement. There is never a concern about the way any stakeholder will be treated in a successful company. When the mission statement

Table 7-1. Central concepts of the mission statements of selected U.S. companies.

Company	Concepts
3M	• Innovation; "thou shalt not kill a new product idea" • Absolute integrity • Respect for individual initiative and personal growth • Tolerance for honest mistakes • Product quality and reliability
American Express	• Heroic customer service • Worldwide reliability of services • Encouragement of individual initiative
Ford	• People as the source of our strength • Products as the "end result of our efforts" (we are *about* cars) • Profits as a necessary means and measure for our success • Basic honesty and integrity
General Electric	• Improving the quality of life through technology and innovation • Interdependent balance between responsibility to customers, employees, society, and shareholders (no clear hierarchy) • Individual responsibility and opportunity • Honesty and integrity
Marriott	• Friendly service and excellent value (customers are guests); "Make people away from home feel that they're among friends and really wanted" • People are number one—treat them well, expect a lot, and the rest will follow • Work hard, yet keep it fun • Continual self-improvement • Overcoming adversity to build character
Procter & Gamble	• Product excellence • Continuous self-improvement • Honesty and fairness • Respect and concern for the individual
Wal-Mart	• "We exist to provide to our customers"—to make their lives better via lower prices and greater selection; all else is secondary • Swim upstream, buck conventional wisdom • Be in partnership with employees • Work with passion, commitment, and enthusiasm • Run lean • Pursue ever-higher goals

Source: Adapted from James C. Collins and Jerry I. Porras, *Built to Last*, New York, HarperCollins, 2002.

embodies these four concepts consistently over time, employees will take ownership and make the commitment necessary to ensure the company is successful regardless of the hours needed.

This mission statement sets the stage for the development of a set of core company values that need to be practiced daily by everyone in the organization. Core values of great companies are very similar and center around such things as servicing customers, high-quality products and services, integrity in all activities, respect for employees, focusing on all the stakeholders, continually being innovative, and contributing to society. The entrepreneur and his or her management team need to make sure that the core values of the company are known and followed. This means that the values are continuously reinforced and reflected in the actions of the company at all levels.

Without the entrepreneur establishing this clearly articulated set of values, he or she cannot expect employees' trust and support of the company and its mission. It takes a long time to establish this trust and commitment, which can be totally lost in just one single act.

The set of core values underpin the purpose of the company—the ultimate reason for its existence. Every company has a core purpose of which every employee must clearly and fully be aware. Examples of a core purpose for some companies follow:

Hewlett-Packard: to make technical contributions for the advancement and welfare of humanity
Mary Kay: to give unlimited opportunity to women
McKinsey: to help leading corporations and governments be more successful
Merck: to preserve and improve human life
Wal-Mart: to give ordinary people the chance to buy the same things as anyone else
Walt Disney: to make people happy

The mission, core values, and purpose are the foundations of every company. Every policy, strategy practice, and tactic should be governed by and support them.

Care needs to be taken to separate the established core values and purpose from best practices and strategies. For example, IBM at one point believed its strategy of mainframe computers was its core value. This idea, for a period of time, wrecked havoc on IBM's market position as it delayed its response to the smaller personal computers coming into the market. Once the core values and strategies were separated and IBM went back to its basic core values, the company responded to this competitive threat with its own version of a small personal computer and reversed its downward trend.

BUILDING STRONG BRANDS

In order to create a lasting company, it is important that the entrepreneur build a strong brand and company identity. A strong brand identification and image can become one of the strongest assets of the entrepreneur's company. Just look at the value of such strong brand and company names like Coca-Cola, Crest, IBM, Intel, Marlboro, Nike, and Saab. Saab is particularly a unique situation as the company has lost significant market share in the last few years by not bringing out new sedans, sports cars, and sport utility vehicles like its competition—Audi, BMW, and Mercedes. General Motors bought 50 percent of Saab for $660 million in 1990 but did little to revitalize the company due to GM's lack of financial ability in the ensuing decade. GM also needed to focus on its own trucks and sport utility vehicles in order to remain competitive. The problems with Saab continued, costing GM significant amounts of revenue until the company bought the remaining 50 percent of Saab for only $50 million—less than 10 percent of the original 50 percent purchase price. Now General Motors is ready to take advantage of Saab's brand name and loyal customer base and will introduce a new Saab based on the concept car in 2004 and a sport utility vehicle the following year. Saab has such strong brand equity that it will allow the rebuilding of the company and its sales based on its past performance.

What is brand equity? Brand equity is a combination of assets and liabilities associated with the name and symbol of the brand that contribute to the value of the product and service with respect to the company and its customers. The assets contributing to this brand equity are brand awareness, brand loyalty, and perceived quality of the product and/or service. An entrepreneur will want to measure the brand equity on a periodic basis to see if he or she is building a brand over time that continues to increase in value. This brand building requires the right combination of advertising, personal selling, packaging, services, and other sales promotional activity that focus on customer satisfaction, which develops into brand loyalty. An entrepreneur can build a strong brand by identifying the most important aspects of building brand equity and then implementing a strategy for building and protecting the brand equity of the product.

Once a strong brand equity and strong market position have been established, the entrepreneur can begin introducing new products, either within the product line or in other categories. Most entrepreneurs use the brand equity to expand the product line and/or extend the brand. When an entrepreneur expands the product line, it means he or she is adding one or more products to an existing product line. This can take the form of adding flavors and other features such as the new cherry supreme cake mix in the Duncan Hines Cake Mix line or Taster's Choice Decaffeinated Coffee to join Taster's Choice Regular (Caffeinated) Coffee.

Another thing the entrepreneur can do is to extend the brand, which means leveraging the brand name into other product categories. One of the most successful examples of brand extension was instituted by Con Agra Inc. with its brand, Healthy Choice Foods. The strong brand equity and name "Healthy Choice" was built on a superior line of frozen meals as a healthy food that tastes good. This resulted in a large number of loyal customers, both male and female. The company then extended the strong brand name to cheeses, deli meats, and soups and continues to use it to launch new products, the importance of which was discussed in Chapter 6.

DEVELOPING COMPETENCE

Building a strong company requires that the entrepreneur develop competence within his or her organization. Overall company competence provides the company with the ability to build, combine, and integrate resources into the products and/or services it offers. Some of the company's competencies are distinctive enough to be labeled core competencies, which provide it with significant sustainable competitive advantages over competition. These core competencies offer real benefits to customers and are difficult to imitate.

Competence of the company can be classified along three dimensions: attitudes, knowledge, and know-how. *Attitudes* in terms of behavior, identity, and determination are sometimes overlooked as part of the competence of a company. Yet, they are essential for any individual or company to achieve anything significant. *Knowledge* is the assimilated information and data of the company being able to successfully build the quality products and services from the resources obtained. Finally, *know-how* reflects the skills and capabilities that define the company's ability to act and produce output according to the developed objectives and processes.

Besides these three competencies, which collectively make up what is sometimes called cognitive capabilities, the company must also have competence in terms of tangible and intangible assets (equipment, buildings, products and services, brand equity, software, and customer loyalty); organizational structure (the structural design of the company and its coordinating mechanisms and processes); and company identity (the beliefs, values, and overall culture of the company). The development of these competencies allows the company to continue to operate and survive for a long period of time despite the presence of hypercompetition and economic and governmental instability.

CORPORATE ETHICS

Today, probably more than any other time since the Great Depression, there are numerous corporate transgressions. Corporate malfeasance has reached an all-time high level in an age of excess. The list of corporate offenders is significant: auditors, CEOs, CFOs, members of the board of directors, and stockbrokers. Also impressive is the list of companies involved, such as Adelphia Communications, Arthur Andersen, Enron, Martha Stewart, Tyco, and Xerox. Even though in terms of the total numbers of U.S. companies, these represent a very small percentage, the lack of good ethics is a problem for governmental leaders as well as the economy. To build a strong company, an entrepreneur needs to have and develop in his or her company good ethics and ethical behavior (honesty, integrity, and trust) as well as a company that practices social responsibility, as evidenced by having a family-friendly workplace and ecological sensitivity.

The increase in unethical and irresponsible activities of companies has shown the need for the entrepreneur to adopt compliance and ethics programs to help prevent and detect any corporate misconduct before real harm occurs. This need has also been influenced by outside threats such as new penalties for ethical infractions, new laws and regulations prohibiting activities in the past that were accepted as norms, and the increased use of criminal laws to punish any misconduct including more punitive damage and stricter jail sentences. Probationary oversight of companies that are found guilty is becoming more frequent and can cause significant company distress.

But government penalties and stricter enforcement of the legal system are not the only things that have caused this need for compliance. The penalties of the marketplace are also powerful motivations. Companies with bad reputations are punished through the loss of consumer confidence and therefore less sales. In the capital markets, unethical behavior can lead to investor dissatisfaction that can cause the company's stock to lose value and make it difficult to access both debt and equity financing, which could ultimately lead to bankruptcy. Also, the recruitment of talented managers and employees is more difficult, if not impossible, when company misconduct is known.

But how does the entrepreneur avoid these negatives and prevent wrongdoing from occurring within his or her organization? One way is to implement an effective ethics and social responsibility program. While there is no widely agreed on effective ethics program, there are some common elements in formal corporate programs. First, a usual part of a corporate ethics program is a formal ethics code for the company. This code details the company's expectations regarding ethics. A second component is an ethics communication system, which provides a mechanism for employees to obtain guidance on ethical infractions and to report abuses. Another usual element is an ethics officer or committee. Many companies have established an ethics officer or committee who has the responsibility to coordinate and develop the company's ethical policies, provide ethics education, and evaluate and investigate any reported violations. The final facet of many corporate ethics programs are ethics training programs. These programs help employees at all levels understand and respond to ethical issues.

Each of these elements as well as entire company ethics programs aim at standardizing behavior through evaluation and norms. In this regard, they have limitations for an entrepreneur trying to build a strong company by having solid corporate ethics. It is more important for an ethically based company to have an approach in which ethical behavior is internalized and has a much broader perspective than just a legalistic orientation. An entrepreneurial company in implementing this approach needs to center on two aspects—management and employee participation. There is no question that the entrepreneur and the management team have to, at the very least, take the lead in developing sound ethical behavior in the company. While they have to take the initiative to develop an ethics program, more importantly they have to set an example for such behavior in their actions both inside and outside the organization. Secondly, this ethics-oriented management team has to develop a participative organization. In a participative organization, the employees have the authority to establish the ethical standards and in fact decide their company environment. This authority is an essential condition for responsible ethical behavior throughout the company. The entrepreneur must move away from the typical command and control management style and adopt a participative, empowerment style of management that allows the establishment of a responsible, ethical organization from within.

DEVELOPING YOUR LEADERSHIP STYLE

As identified in Chapter 1, to build a strong company the entrepreneur must develop a leadership and management style that allows this to occur while establishing an information system that provides timely information needed for sound decision making, particularly in those areas identified as critical for future success. Besides having a vision, being a risk taker and encourager, and adopting an intrapreneurial style of management, all discussed in previous chapters, two other aspects of this leadership style for developing a strong company need to be specifically mentioned: building trust and empowering. Building trust, or reliance, by one person, group, or company with others to recognize and protect the rights and interests of all engaged in the same joint endeavor, is essential for an entrepreneur. A high level of trust in a company reflects that everyone involved understands that successful cooperation in realizing the vision and direction of the company will also serve their individual rights and interests. In part, trust is what allowed Henry Meyer, chairman and CEO of Key Corp, one of the largest banks in the United States, to slim the bank down after decades of growing through acquisitions. He was able to initiate and implement a restructuring plan that reduced the number of employees nationwide by 4000 and the company businesses from 22 to 10. Henry Meyer is known for the ability to interface so that every individual feels valued. He inspires people to work harder with renewed energy. Building trust requires that the entrepreneur is concerned about and protects the interest of his or her employees while empowering them to want to do their jobs better.

Empowerment is a process whereby an individual employee's belief in his or her self-efficacy is enhanced. It involves the process of decentralizing decision making in the company, with more discretion and autonomy being given further down in the organization.

An entrepreneur does not remove him- or herself from making decisions and empowering; nor does he or she turn the company's operations into a democracy. Rather, by empowering employees, an entrepreneur is insisting that employees take personal responsibility for their mistakes and successes.

How can you empower your employees? An entrepreneur can empower his or her employees by providing motivation and support, spending time with employees, giving information and constructive feedback, and constantly reminding them to exercise their decision-making authority. This requires one to relinquish some traditional authority of position and accept feelings of being threatened as these empowered employees become bolder about speaking up and challenging authority. Employees will want more and more responsibility to help fulfill the vision of the company and impact their own destiny. Empowering and developing leaders is what Roger Enrico, chairman and CEO of Pepsi Cola, a nearly $30 billion multibusiness corporation with 300,000 employees, did to develop a world-class, best-practices company. If Henry Meyer and Robert Enrico can do this successfully with their large corporate, bureaucratic structures, an entrepreneur should surely be able to establish trust and empowerment in his or her company. This requires that the entrepreneur be confident but not feel invincible.

Care needs to be taken that one does not fall into the same trap as that of the head of Pan American World Airlines, who said publicly that the company could not live without him—and indeed the company no longer exists. Another example of poor employee empowerment practices is seen in the case of one of the greatest innovators and creators of all time, Walt Disney. Walt Disney not only did not groom a successor, he also felt so invincible that he left tapes to be played after his death eliciting the question in many management decision sessions: "What would Walt Disney do?" The company floundered for about 15 years after Walt Disney's death and was almost acquired by a Japanese company. These two cases indicate the necessity of recognizing vulnerability and engaging in sound succession planning.

SUCCESSION PLANNING

To build a strong, lasting company, an entrepreneur needs to put into place basic operating mechanisms and people who will continue growth and improvement in the company. Comparing the start-up and growth of Zenith and Motorola illustrates this. Both companies were founded about the same time by entrepreneurs who died 18 months apart. The entrepreneurs had two very different leadership styles, which are reflected in their companies today. The founder of Zenith was very charismatic but did not build his organization structure and carefully groom his replacement to continue after his death. Today Zenith is still doing the same thing—mostly producing appliances. The Motorola founder was different. While not being as charismatic, he built an organizational structure and groomed his replacement so that today Motorola is world-class and active in new markets and products such as cellular phones. A key aspect of the difference in the two companies is succession planning.

Succession planning involves everything from recruiting the right candidate to developing new leadership from within. It is more than just the organizational plan that was an essential element of your original business plan, showing who holds what job within the company. Succession planning allows a company to align its business goals and vision with its human capital needs by developing, motivating, and retaining top leadership that has the necessary skills and competencies to lead and manage the company in the hypercompetitive global environment of today, as well as in the future.

Succession planning is all about business continuation and people. Its purpose is to ensure business continuity from one leader to the next, and as such, should be a formal, on-going process of identifying, assessing, and developing talent.

In terms of the replacement of the entrepreneur, succession planning requires that the specific skills and competencies needed by the successor are identified; the process for grooming the successor is developed; individuals within (or outside) the company who will be considered are identified; and the transition process and how it will be communicated to internal and external stakeholders is implemented. An exemplary succession plan took place at General Electric when Jack Welch stepped down and chose his successor. Similar effective succession planning occurred for American International Group for its highly visible chairman and CEO, Maurice "Hank" Greenberg. While not without challenges and problems, sound succession planning coupled with sustaining core values, building strong brands, developing competencies, having ethical behavior, and implementing the right leadership style helps an entrepreneur build a strong company that will last.

PART II

MARKETING PROBLEMS

8

Focusing on a Market Niche and Customer

PROFILE—STANLEY MARCUS

One of the most well known retail entrepreneurs is Stanley Marcus, who grew Nieman Marcus into one of the world's best-recognized, successful specialty department stores. While Stanley Marcus has many interesting stories dealing with customers at the retail level, perhaps his most famous one occurred in his dealing with a customer return with his father, Herbert, a founder of the business. A customer purchased a dress from Nieman Marcus. When she demanded her money back Stanley Marcus was resistant, as he knew he was being abused by the woman, who had worn and ruined the dress; with this being the case, the manufacturer of the dress would not help pay for it. Stanley's father, Herbert, admonished his son for resisting, saying that the woman was dealing with the Nieman Marcus store, not the manufacturer, and should get her money back with no questions asked. Herbert did not want to lose a customer over a $175 dress. As the story goes, someone calculated that the woman went on to spend over $500,000 at Nieman Marcus as a satisfied customer, not an unhappy one. Even though the store may have been taken advantage of, things of this nature sometimes occur in operating a business. While the customer may not always be right, an entrepreneur should *always* let them think they are.

Stanley Marcus received a very valuable lesson in growing a business—each and every customer should be the focus of attention and should be treated properly. This lesson should be the focus of all entrepreneurial activities particularly in these difficult, hypercompetitive times. According to one survey, 96 percent of dissatisfied customers complain to an average of nine other people instead of to the organization causing the complaint. This compounds the problem of a dissatisfied customer, considering that if this dissatisfaction causes the customer not to do any more business with the company, it will cost the company an average of six times more to attract a new customer than to keep the existing one. This chapter focuses on avoiding the mistakes of not defining and focusing on market niche and customer satisfaction by discussing market niching, market segmentation, market gridding, and customer value and satisfaction.

MARKET NICHING

The concept of market niching is probably the most important aspect of marketing an entrepreneur should consider when starting a company. At the heart of this concept is the market itself. But what exactly is a market? What criteria should be used in selecting one?

There are different types of markets—national and local markets, export and domestic markets, stock markets, furniture markets, wholesale and retail markets, and many more too numerous to mention.

Generally, a market occurs when buyers and sellers assemble, goods are offered for sale at prices and conditions that buyers accept, and a transfer of title occurs. The criteria used in defining a good market are (1) measurability, (2) accessibility, (3) profitability, and (4) stability.

The *measurability* criterion indicates the degree to which the size and other aspects of the market can be determined (measured). Certain markets are very difficult to measure. For example, it is very difficult to determine the number of people who wear sandals who would prefer a new rope sandal style. The *accessibility* criterion refers to the company's capability of effectively marketing and delivering the product to the defined market segment. Even though the results of the segmentation process may look impressive, a market segment that cannot be profitably reached is not of any value to the entrepreneur. The *profitability* criterion indicates whether the defined segment is large enough to be worthwhile by producing sufficient sales and profits. It is important that the size of the market segment justify the effort and expense of successfully reaching and serving it. For example, it may not be worthwhile for an entrepreneur to develop clothes and shoes only for women who are very tall. Finally, the political *stability* of the market segment, both now and in the future, should be favorable. There is no return in investing a large amount of time, money, and energy in a country only to have the operation shut down or nationalized at a later date.

By using the specific criteria established to identify several market alternatives, the best market can then be selected by the entrepreneur for the particular product or service to achieve the best possible sales and profits. Sales and profits can result from a variety of strategies, such as (1) a change in the marketing strategy (the Arm & Hammer baking soda line increased sales using a new selling concept—using the product for whitening teeth); (2) a change in the size of packages (many canners of fruits and vegetables have added product sales by adding a very large can size previously only used in institutions such as restaurants and hotels); (3) a change in the communications system for reaching a market (Polymer Technology promoted its Boston Lens contact lens solutions in the Canadian market through flyers, price deals, trade advertising, and market representatives); and (4) a change in the geographical area(s) that was not in the original market (Puerto Rico, Trinidad, and many other Caribbean islands now sell Uncle Ben's Rice even though none of these markets was a part of the original marketing plan).

MARKET SEGMENTATION TECHNIQUES

The process of defining and selecting the right market niche—market segmentation—is extremely important for the success of an entrepreneur, particularly in the start-up phase of the new venture. Once the target market has been correctly defined, it is much easier to develop a marketing strategy and the appropriate combination of product, distribution, promotion, and price to reach that market effectively.

Table 8-1. Market segmentation techniques by type of market.

Segmentation Criteria	**Basis for Type of Market**		
	Consumer	***Industrial***	***Government***
Demographic	Age, family size, education level, family life cycle, income, nationality, occupation, race, religion, residence, sex, social class	Number of employees, size of sales, size of profit, type of product line	Type of agency, size of budget, amount of autonomy
Geographic	Region of country, city, size, market density, climate	Region of country	Federal, state, local
Psychological	Lifestyle personality traits, motives	Degree of industrial leadership	Degree of forward thinking
Benefits	Durability, dependability, economy, esteem enhancement of earnings, status from ownership	Dependability, reliability of seller and support service, efficiency in operation or use, enhancement of firm's earnings, durability	Dependability, reliability of seller and support services
Volume of Use	Heavy, medium, light	Heavy, medium, light	Heavy, medium, light
Controllable Marketing Elements	Sales promotion, price, advertising, guarantee, warranty, retail store purchased service, product attributes, reputation of seller	Price, service, warranty, reputation of seller	Price, reputation of seller

Source: Robert D. Hisrich, *Marketing*, 2nd ed., Hauppauge, N.Y.: Barron's Educational Series, 2000, p. 77.

The overall segmentation techniques for all three types of markets (consumer, industrial, and government) are indicated in Table 8-1. The basic segmentation criteria—demographic, geographic, psychological, benefits, volume of use, and controllable marketing elements—can be effectively used to define a market niche regardless of whether the overall market is consumer, industrial, or government. Not only will these segmentation techniques define the market niche, but they also help construct the market plan to successfully sell to the market niche identified.

Geographic Segmentation

One of the most widely used segmentation techniques is dividing the market into separate geographic clusters such as nations, regions, states, cities, or localities. Census information on both businesses and consumers as well as data from trade associations and publications is broken down on a geographic basis, allowing market size to be more easily determined. In geographic segmentation, an entrepreneur can choose a market where there is a comparative advantage in terms of such marketing variables as distribution, advertising, and/or company image. For example, one producer of specialty oil and fat products for commercial bakeries and restaurants expanded its marketing into the New England and New York area because of the cost advantages in transportation from a Pennsylvania plant location close to these areas.

Demographic Segmentation

When you determine that there are particular types of individuals or companies that are more likely to use a product, you are defining a market through demographic segmentation. Even though demographics is not the only way to define a market niche, it is the most widely used market segmentation method. This method is frequently used because the demographic variables are often closely associated with expenditure and preference patterns, the variables are easy to measure, and there is significant published information available. This data is readily available in a published form from such sources as the

U.S. Census. When original published data is not available, then primary research can be used to determine the best market niche. For industrial products, this can involve interviewing an individual of a company to determine if the company is the appropriate market niche for the entrepreneur. Some of the most frequently used variables in demographic segmentation for each of the three markets are indicated in Table 8-1.

Psychological Segmentation

Although there are many different psychological segmentation variables that can be used (see Table 8-1), the three most common in the consumer market are lifestyle, motives, and personality traits. When psychological variables are used in market segmentation, primary research is almost always required because little, if any, published data exist on these variables.

When using lifestyle segmentation, the market niche is being evaluated on the basis of attitudes on consumption, work, and play. Even though lifestyle segmentation usually requires significant expenditure on research, it is increasingly being used to identify market niches. Volkswagen, for example, introduced what it termed 'life-styled' automobiles—an economical Volkswagen for conservative drivers and a sportier model for car buffs.

Motives are another commonly used psychological variable. Since motives move an individual toward a goal, they may influence a person's purchasing behavior. Motives can vary from emotional ones (prestige, belonging, love) to economic ones (product dependability, affordability, and convenience). For example, if convenience is the primary motivating factor, then the number of stores that carry the entrepreneur's product become extremely important.

Benefit Segmentation

Perhaps the most important segmentation method for defining the market niche and developing the right marketing plan for successful sales is benefit segmentation—identifying the various benefits potential customers expect from the particular product. Consumers are identified according to the importance of the different benefits they are looking for from the specific product being investigated. For example, one group of automobile buyers identified may be seeking a car that has the following product benefits: economical to maintain, easy to operate, and inexpensive to purchase and repair.

Various general benefits can be used in the consumer market, such as durability, dependability, convenience, and the status that derives from ownership. Although some criteria, such as dependability and durability, are useful in segmenting the industrial and government market for new products, other criteria are frequently more important in these markets. For example, the buyer of a new product in the industrial market may be looking for reliability in the seller and support services, efficiency in operation, and/or enhancement of the firm's earnings. Of course, determining very specific benefits for your product or service is best. The entrepreneur must take care to ensure that the benefits identified are also the real reasons underlying the product purchase decision. Although home gardeners may indicate that they buy a particular new brand of fertilizer for ecological reasons, the real reason may be economy.

Volume Segmentation

In volume segmentation, the market niche is defined on a use/nonuse basis. Even more important, the use in the segment can be further classified by the amount of product consumed; the users of the entrepreneur's product can be divided either according to heavy, medium, or light usage, or even better, by the actual amount consumed each week or each month.

Controllable Marketing Elements

Another frequently used segmentation technique is controllable marketing elements. The entrepreneur divides the market based on the responsiveness to different marketing elements within the firm's control such as price, advertising, sales promotion, warranty, guarantee, or service. As indicated in Table 8-1 the most important marketing elements will vary by type of market—consumer, industrial, or government. The elements identified as important in any of the markets should receive the most emphasis in the introductory marketing plan.

Brand Loyalty Segmentation

Brand loyalty, the strength of preference a customer has for one brand over another, indicates the tendency of a customer to purchase a particular brand on a regular basis. In using brand loyalty as a segmentation technique, the amount of brand loyalty is indicated by its relative position versus other brands in the product/market space. Brand loyalty also varies greatly by product category. For example, canned vegetables generally have low brand loyalty. Toothpaste is a product category with high brand loyalty, where consumers do not switch brands very often. A similar wide variation in brand loyalty occurs in service industries. While beauty salons and banks generally have high brand loyalty, a laundromat has low brand loyalty. Markets with a high degree of brand loyalty are more difficult for the entrepreneur to enter and require even more specific market niching and marketing efforts for successful entry.

Product Segmentation

Product segmentation can be used by the entrepreneur to uncover a unique market niche and opportunity. Usually, consumer preference for a product along some key dimension of the product is distributed along a normal curve. This leaves smaller, sometimes unexploited markets at the extremes of this normal curve, since most manufacturers aim at the larger markets, found at the median or center of the normal curve. For example, most manufacturers want to include just the proper amount of chocolate in their chocolate cakes so as to satisfy the majority of the population. Consumers who desire a strong chocolate flavor and consumers who like a light chocolate flavor are at opposite ends of the curve and are often ignored, even though they represent a viable unexploited market.

New opportunities are also found by asking consumers to calculate how close each brand is to every other brand. Whenever a proposed new product is found that has preference over existing brands, this proposed product can be developed to conform to the consumers' perception of what it should be.

MARKET GRIDDING

A useful technique for the entrepreneur in identifying a good market niche is market gridding. A market grid depicts the total market in a two- or three-dimensional manner, based on selected relevant market characteristics. An example of a market grid for a new commercial bank is shown in Table 8-2. Potential customers in the target market are shown in the lined area; customers who are not a part of the potential market but who are a part of the total market are in the "all others" category. This analysis of the industrial market as the potential target market for the commercial bank uses a demographic segmentation variable (type of business) and a controllable marketing element segment variable (services that could be offered by the bank). This grid attempts to determine the amount of use each type of business would have for each of the potential services of the bank.

CUSTOMER VALUE AND SATISFACTION

Once a market niche is identified, every effort of the entrepreneur and the company should be centered on creating customer satisfaction. Customer satisfaction is the extent to which an entrepreneurial company fulfills a customer's needs, desires, and expectations. This satisfaction of the entrepreneur's target customers at a profit is the heart of the marketing concept. When using the marketing concept, the customer becomes the dominant focal point of the firm, with all the resources and activities in the firm directed at generating customer satisfaction.

How is customer satisfaction obtained? First, the entrepreneur needs to focus continuously on developing new quality products. It is important that the firm stand solidly behind each new product

Table 8-2. Market Grid Examples for the Services of a New Commercial Bank for the Industrial Market.

Bank Service / Type of Business	Insurance and Real Estate	Construction	Wholesale Trade	Utilities	Transportation	Service Industries	Retail Trade	Manufacturing
Commercial loans								
Checking accounts								
Savings accounts								
Safe-deposit box								
Branch banking								
After-hours depository								
Bank-by-mail								
Lock-box plan								
Account reconcilement plan								
Freight payment plan								
Payroll accounting plan								
All others								

through the use of a warranty or guarantee. A strong warranty or guarantee assures each customer that he or she does not have to worry whether the product will perform as expected.

Another way is for the entrepreneur to provide superior customer service. One clothing store in Connecticut, Michells of Westport, is known for its superior customer service. If a customer calls after hours, the call is forwarded to the home of one of the owners. They will go to the store after hours and help the customer obtain any item needed. Every employee in the store knows the names of each customer, their business, and the name(s) of the spouse and children. The store has a big area for customers waiting for alterations and for entertaining children. No wonder its customers are so satisfied and return to the store for their clothing needs. As A. Malachi Mixon III, a successful entrepreneur who is president and CEO of Invacare Corporation, stated, "As you grow, be aware of your size and make sure you do not lose your response time to your customers. You do not want to become a lumbering elephant instead of an agile antelope." How does an entrepreneur accomplish this? By focusing on the customer and market niche of a new product or service, an entrepreneur can reap the benefits of a successful venture.

9

Going International

PROFILE—STEVE LAMOND

Steve Lamond launched Turbine Systems Inc. in 1992 in Warehouse Point, Connecticut, to overhaul and repair oil field equipment overseas, beginning in the northern Africa region. The new venture had all the aspects of being very successful: an interested client who needed help overhauling and repairing equipment used in its Algerian oil fields, and a father who had extensive knowledge of and experience in northern Africa. For the first year and a half, the projects were financed by cash from both Steve and his father. But as business started to grow and accelerate it became clear to Steve that this source of financing would not be enough to support the growth. Financing for a global service company is not easy to obtain, as Steve soon found out when he began to explore his financial options. For any small business without sales and successful projects to back up its validity and create a positive track record of sales and profits, it is difficult to obtain financing. Financing becomes even more difficult for a small business doing business internationally. And if the international arena of the business is volatile, it is almost impossible.

One method for obtaining financing in this situation is by factoring accounts receivable, which is what Steve Lamond used to finance Turbine Systems Inc. at the start of its growth. When the

$4 million company had no other traditional credit available, another source of financing was found that is available for all companies doing business overseas — government guaranteed loans. The Export-Import Bank provided insurance against default by foreign creditors as a guarantee for working capital loans. Since some contracts have a 6-month to 1-year delivery period, this guarantee allowed Turbine Systems Inc. to borrow money against confirmed letters of credit from foreign buyers to buy parts, build products, ship the products, and collect from the letters of credit.

With a significant interest in global activities and more of a global view of the U.S. economy occurring than previously, more entrepreneurs and smaller businesses also are interested in being involved in international business activity. Yet few entrepreneurs are as fortunate as Steve Lamond to successfully engage in international entrepreneurship.

What is international entrepreneurship? It is the process of an entrepreneur conducting business activities across national boundaries. It may consist of exporting, licensing, opening a sales office in another country, or something as simple as placing a classified advertisement in the Paris edition of the *Herald Tribune.* The activities necessary for ascertaining and satisfying the needs and wants of target consumers often take place in more than one country. When an entrepreneur executes his or her business in more than one country, international entrepreneurship is occurring.

INTERNATIONAL VERSUS DOMESTIC ENTREPRENEURSHIP

Although international and domestic entrepreneurs alike are concerned with sales, costs, and profits, what differentiates domestic from international entrepreneurship is the variation in the relative importance of the factors involved in each decision. International entrepreneurial decisions are more complex due to such uncontrollable factors as economics, politics, culture, and technology. Since specific regulations and trade practices may differ greatly from the entrepreneurship's originating country, it is imperative for the entrepreneur to be aware of the many additional facets of expanding a business globally.

Economics

When an entrepreneur designs a domestic business strategy, a single country at a specified level of economic development is the focus of these efforts. Creating a business strategy for a multicountry area means dealing with differences in levels of economic development; currency valuations; government regulations; and banking, economic, marketing, and distribution systems. These differences manifest themselves in each aspect of the entrepreneur's international business plan and methods of doing business.

Stage of Economic Development

The United States is an industrially developed nation with regional variances. While needing to adjust the business plan according to regional differences, an entrepreneur doing business only in the United States does not have to worry about a significant lack of such fundamental infrastructures as roads, electricity, communication systems, banking facilities and systems, adequate educational systems, a well-developed legal system, and established business ethics and norms. These factors vary greatly in other countries, from those that have industrialized to those in the process of developing.

Balance of Payments

With the present system of flexible exchange rates, a country's balance of payments (the difference between the value of a country's imports and exports over time) affects the valuation of currency. The valuation of one country's currency affects how companies in that country do business in other countries. At one time, Italy's chronic balance of payments deficit led to a radical depreciation in the value of the lira, the currency of Italy. Fiat responded by offering significant rebates on cars sold in the United States. These rebates cost Fiat very little due to the decrease in the value of the lira.

Type of System

Pepsi-Cola began considering the possibility of marketing in the former USSR as early as 1959, during then U.S. Vice President Richard Nixon's visit there. When Premier Nikita Khrushchev expressed his approval of Pepsi's taste, the slow wheels of East-West trade began moving, with Pepsi entering the former USSR 13 years later. Instead of using its traditional type of franchise bottler system in this entry, Pepsi used a barter-type arrangement that satisfied both the socialized system of the former USSR and the U.S. capitalist system. In return for receiving technology and syrup from Pepsi, the former USSR provided the company with Soviet vodka and the right to distribute it in the United States.

There are many difficulties in doing business in developing and transition economies. These problems reflect the gaps in the basic knowledge of the Western system regarding business plans, product promotion, marketing, and profits; widely variable rates of return; nonconvertibility of the currency, which necessitates finding a countertrade item; differences in the accounting system; and nightmarish communications.

Political-Legal Environment

The multiplicity of political and legal environments in the international market creates vastly different business problems, opening some market opportunities for entrepreneurs and eliminating others. Each element of the business strategy of an international entrepreneur has the potential to be affected by the multiplicity of legal environments. Pricing decisions in a country that has a value-added tax are different from those decisions made by the same entrepreneur in a country with no value-added tax. Advertising strategy is affected by the variations in what can be said in the copy or in the support needed for advertising claims in different countries. Product decisions are affected by legal requirements with respect to labeling, ingredients, and packaging. Types of ownership and organizational forms also vary widely throughout the world.

Cultural Environment

The impact of culture on entrepreneurs and strategies is also significant. Entrepreneurs must make sure that each element in the business plan has some degree of congruence with the local culture. For example, in some countries, point-of-purchase displays are not allowed in retail stores as they are in the United States. Some cultures provide a specific opportunity for new ventures, as in the case of Eric Hautemont, a Frenchman who founded Ray Dream Inc. in California.

Technological Environment

Technology, like culture, varies significantly across countries. The variations and availability of technology are often surprising, particularly to an entrepreneur from a developed country like the United States. Many Americans, for example, have a difficult time understanding how a technologically advanced military economy like the former USSR could have had shortages of food and consumer goods and an almost Third World communication system.

New products in a country are created based on the conditions and infrastructure operant in that country. For example, U.S. car designers can assume wider roads and less expensive gasoline than can European designers. When these same designers work on transportation vehicles for other parts of the world, their assumptions need to be significantly altered.

DOING INTERNATIONAL BUSINESS

As indicated in Table 9-1, there are various ways an entrepreneur can become involved in international business and begin to market and service products internationally. The method of entry into a market and the mode of operating overseas are dependent on the goals of the entrepreneur and his or her company's strengths and weaknesses. The modes of entering or engaging in international business can be divided into several categories.

Table 9-1. Methods for doing international business.

Exporting
a. Indirect Exporting
   1. Foreign purchaser in a local market
   2. Export management firm
b. Direct Exporting
   1. Independent foreign distributors
   2. Overseas sales office

Nonequity Arrangements
a. Licensing
b. Turn-Key Projects
c. Management Contracts

Direct Foreign Investment
a. Minority Interests
b. Joint Ventures
c. Majority Interests

Exporting

As a general rule, an entrepreneur starts doing international business through exporting. Exporting normally involves the sale and shipping of products manufactured in one country to a customer located in another country. There are two general classifications of exporting: direct and indirect.

Indirect Exporting

Indirect exporting involves having a foreign purchaser in the local market or using an export management firm. For certain commodities and manufactured goods, foreign buyers actively seek out sources of supply and have purchasing offices in markets throughout the world. An entrepreneur wanting to sell into one of these overseas markets can deal with one of these buyers. In this case, the entire transaction is handled as though it were a domestic transaction, even though the goods will be shipped out of the country. This method of exporting involves the least amount of knowledge and risk for the entrepreneur.

Export management firms, another method of indirect exporting, are located in most commercial centers. For a fee, these firms will provide representation in foreign markets. Typically, they represent a group of noncompeting manufacturers from the same country who have no interest in becoming directly involved in exporting. The export management firm handles all of the selling, marketing, and distribution, in addition to any technical problem involved in the export process.

Direct Exporting

If the entrepreneur wants more involvement without any financial commitment, direct exporting through independent distributors, or the company's own overseas sales office, is a way to get involved in international business. Independent foreign distributors usually handle products for firms seeking relatively rapid entry into a large number of foreign markets. This independent distributor directly contacts foreign customers and potential customers and takes care of all the technicalities of arranging for export documentation, financing, and delivery for an established rate of commission.

Entrepreneurs who do not wish to submit to the loss of control over their marketing efforts that occurs when using independent distributors can open their own overseas sales offices and hire their own salespeople to provide market representation. In starting out, the entrepreneur may send a U.S. or domestic salesperson to be a representative in the foreign market. As more business is done in the overseas sales in the foreign market, warehouses are usually opened, followed by a local assembly process when sales reach a level high enough to warrant the investment. The assembly operation eventually can evolve into the establishment of manufacturing operations in the foreign market. Entrepreneurs then export the output from these manufacturing operations to other international markets.

Nonequity Arrangements

When market and financial conditions warrant the change, an entrepreneur can enter into international business by one of three types of nonequity arrangements: licensing, turn-key projects, and management contracts. Each of these allows the entrepreneur to enter a market and obtain sales and profits without direct equity investment in the foreign market. Entrepreneurs who either cannot export or make direct investments or who simply choose not to engage in those activities still have the possibility of doing international business through nonequity arrangements.

Licensing

Licensing involves an entrepreneur who is a manufacturer (licensee) giving a foreign manufacturer (licensor) the right to use a patent, trademark, technology, production process, or product in return for the payment of a royalty. The licensing arrangement is most appropriate when the entrepreneur has no intention of entering a particular market through exporting or direct investment. Since the process is low-risk, yet provides a way to generate incremental income, a licensing arrangement can be a good method for the entrepreneur to engage in international business. Unfortunately, some entrepreneurs have entered into these arrangements without careful analysis and have later found that they have licensed their largest competitor into business or that they are investing large sums of time and money in helping the licensor adopt the technology or know-how being licensed.

Wolverine World Wide, Inc. opened a Hush Puppies store in Sofia, Bulgaria, through a licensing agreement with Pikin, a combine. Similar arrangements were made a year later in the former USSR with Kirov, a shoe combine. The stores have done well through these licensing arrangements.

Turn-Key Projects

Another method by which the entrepreneur can gain some international business experience without much risk is through turn-key projects. The underdeveloped or lesser-developed countries have recognized their need for manufacturing technology and infrastructure and yet do not want to turn over substantial portions of their economy to foreign ownership. One solution to this dilemma has been to have a foreign entrepreneur build a factory or other facility, train the workers to operate the equipment, train the management to run the installation, and then turn it over to local owners once the operation is going; hence the name *turn-key operation*.

Entrepreneurs have found the turn-key project an attractive alternative. Initial profits can be made from this method, and follow-up export sales can result. Financing is often provided by the local company or government, with periodic payments being made over the life of the project.

Management Contracts

A final nonequity method the entrepreneur can use in international business is the management contract. Several entrepreneurs have successfully entered international business by contracting their management techniques and managerial skills. These contracts sometimes follow a turn-key project, where the foreign owner wants to use the management of the turn-key supplier.

The management contract allows the purchasing country to obtain foreign expertise without giving ownership of its resources to a foreigner. For the entrepreneur, the management contract is another way of entering foreign markets that would otherwise be closed, and of obtaining a profit without a large equity investment.

Direct Foreign Investment

The wholly owned foreign subsidiary has been the preferred mode of ownership for entrepreneurs using a direct foreign investment for doing business in international markets. Joint ventures and minority and majority equity positions are also methods for making direct foreign investments. The percentage of ownership obtained in the foreign venture by the entrepreneur is related to nationality, the amount of overseas experience, the nature of the industry, and the rules of the host government.

Japanese companies have been frequent users of the minority equity position in direct foreign investment. A *minority interest* can provide a firm with a source of raw materials or a relatively captive market for its products. Entrepreneurs have used minority positions to gain a foothold or acquire experience in a market before making a major commitment. When the minority shareholder has something of strong value, the ability to influence the decision-making process is often far in excess of the shareholding.

Another equity method that allows the entrepreneur to enter international markets is the purchasing of a *majority interest* in a foreign business. In a technical sense, anything over 50 percent of the equity in a firm is majority interest. The majority interest allows the entrepreneur to obtain managerial control while maintaining the acquired firm's local identity. When entering a volatile international market, some entrepreneurs take a smaller position that they increase up to 100 percent as sales and profits occur. This practice, often enforced according to regulatory restrictions imposed by many countries out of concern for the rights of minority shareholders, is a means of reducing possible conflict with the local owner.

An entrepreneur using 100 percent ownership to engage in international business assures complete control. Many U.S. entrepreneurs have the desire for complete ownership and control in cases of foreign investments. If the entrepreneur has the capital, technology, and marketing skills required for successful entry into a market, there may be no reason to share ownership.

Another direct foreign investment method used by entrepreneurs to enter foreign markets is the *joint venture*. Although a joint venture can take on many forms, in its most traditional form, two firms (for example, one U.S. firm and one German firm) get together and form a third company in which they share the equity.

Joint ventures have been used by entrepreneurs most often in two situations: (1) when the entrepreneur wants to purchase local knowledge as well as an already-established marketing or manufacturing facility, and (2) when rapid entry into a market is needed. Sometimes joint ventures are eventually dissolved by the entrepreneur taking 100 percent ownership.

MARKETING STRATEGIES

In transferring a product from one country to another, one of the most difficult areas is cross-national advertising. Some companies handle all issues of international advertising at corporate headquarters. For example, a company advertising in Switzerland obtains some advertising coverage in Italy, France, and Germany. In most border areas, consumers understand the neighboring country's language because distances are short and continual interaction occurs between citizens.

You should keep in mind that subsidiaries in various countries usually do not have a worldwide vision. They are not concerned about the advantages of advertising overlap and therefore are not concerned about making their advertising available to affiliated companies in contingent countries. Since it is very difficult to obtain a 100 percent, legally safe trade name that is meaningful in many different languages, you should not put forth excessive effort in this area. Instead, you should attempt to develop a nonmeaningful trade name—a new word, really—as Kodak, Exxon, and so many others have done. The value in this type of trade name occurs when subsidiaries use it on brands being sold.

BARRIERS TO INTERNATIONAL ENTREPRENEURSHIP

Often governments influence trade to accomplish certain economic, political, and/or social objectives of the country. This can even take the form of a group of governments such as the European Union (EU), the North America Free Trade Agreement (NAFTA), or the Free Trade Area (FTA). When countries band together to increase trade and investment between them to the exclusion of countries outside the group, a trade bloc is formed.

There are several reasons for government intervention in trade. These include preventing unemployment, protecting infant industries, promoting industrialization of the country, maintaining essential industries, dealing with unfriendly countries, preserving national identity, and maintaining influence. Since any intervention in trade by a government, regardless of its cause, can cause retaliation from other governments, it is useful for the entrepreneur when accessing international market opportunities to understand the barriers that will occur in the particular country context.

Tariffs

One method for affecting prices of foreign goods directly is by levying a tariff on a product or product category. A tariff (sometimes called *duty*), the most common type of trade control, is a tax levied by the government on a good shipped internationally. If the tax is collected by the exporting country, it is an export tariff. If the tax is collected by the importing country, it is an import tariff, the most common tariff. Regardless of the type, a tariff raises the price of the good to the purchaser.

Since import tariffs are the ones that most concern the entrepreneur, it is important to understand their effect on your product or service competing in that particular country's marketplace. By raising the price of your product, a tariff on your product gives domestically produced goods a relative price advantage, while providing revenue to the government of the country. Even if there are no competing domestic products, the tariff raises the price of your product, making it less desirable for purchasing by residents of the country; overall, this reduces the amount spent on foreign goods and services.

Other Direct Price Influences

In addition to tariffs, there are other ways a government can directly influence the price of your product—aid and loans, customs valuation, and subsidies. Governments, particularly the U.S. government, give aid and loans to other countries and often require the recipient to spend this money on products and services originating in the donor country. Another way to affect the price is to adjust the custom valuation on goods perceived to be priced arbitrarily low, thereby raising the price in the country. Finally, governments sometimes make direct payments to domestic companies to compensate for any losses occurring from selling abroad.

Nontariff Barriers

Besides affecting price, there are other ways a government can influence trade—by directly controlling the amount of a product or product category that can enter the country. Some of these mechanisms are local legislation, quotas, reciprocal requirements, and standards. Particularly for controlling the amount of goods used, governments prefer to buy goods that are domestically produced or goods that at least contain a certain percentage of locally originated products. This "buy local" legislation makes sure government purchases give preference to locally produced products or services over foreign ones.

Quotas limit the amount of a product that can be imported or exported. When the quota is on the amount of the imports allowed, the government basically guarantees that a certain percentage of the domestic market is for domestic producers. This usually increases the consumer price of the product, as there is little incentive for companies to use price as a means of increasing rates.

Table 9-2. Going international—help for entrepreneurs.

- Global Trade Source Ltd. (www.globaltrade.com) provides a newsletter which contains, among other things, country-specific comments from small business people all over the world about the specific business climate in that country.
- International Trade Administration of the U.S. Department of Commerce (www.ita.doc.gov) provides country guides to almost all export markets and solutions to common trade problems.
- SBA's Export Assistance Centers (www.sba.gov) provide information on centers located throughout the United States that assist entrepreneurs in obtaining export financing, making contacts with potential foreign customers, and providing research on foreign markets.
- Small Business Exporters Association (www.sbea.org) is a national small and midsize businesses trade association providing networking opportunities and assisting in legal challenges of exporting.

Sometimes a government requires an exporter to take merchandise or promise to take goods or services from the country in lieu of cash. These types of reciprocal requirements are often found in certain industries such as aerospace and defense, as well as when an industrialized nation is doing business with a developing one.

Finally, countries establish clarification, labeling, quality, and testing standards that must be met before a product or service will be allowed to be sold in the country. These effectively add to the foreign company's production costs or even eliminate its market entrance because the standards cannot be met.

Regardless of the type of restriction, an entrepreneur must carefully analyze the impact of this restriction when developing a strategy for selecting and entering a global marketplace. If done improperly, going international can be a costly mistake for an entrepreneur, and only through diligence and understanding the process can this mistake be avoided. Some sources of assistance for going international are indicated in Table 9-2.

By understanding the differences in doing domestic and international entrepreneurship, the various modes of doing international business, and the barriers involved, an entrepreneur can create a successful global company.

10

Growing Your Business

PROFILE—IRVING SPARAGE

Irving Sparage's firm, Smith Welding Supply Inc., was finding its location in downtown Detroit, Michigan, too small to accommodate the business and its future growth. The company, which employs 65 workers, was on its way to a $14 million sales year when the recession hit in 2001, and the company had sales significantly less than its 2000 sales level. Regardless of the loss in sales, Irving Sparage decided to move forward with the relocation from downtown Detroit to suburban Ferndale, Michigan, at a cost of about $1 million. The move and growing in the future included investing in high-technology equipment at the new facility and adding 10 new individuals to the sales staff.

Like Irving Sparage, the question facing each entrepreneur after he or she has successfully launched the new venture is, To grow or not to grow? While many entrepreneurs choose not to grow their ventures, for those who choose to expand, it is necessary to prepare and plan for growth and to understand what this means for both the individual entrepreneur and the venture. The impact on the number and duties of the entrepreneur and the management team, the management style of the entrepreneur, the inventory and accounts receivable requirements, the production requirements, and the financial requirements are just a few areas that need to be carefully addressed before a growth strategy is implemented.

In many cases, growth may not be entirely voluntary. Customers may demand more volume, better service, and even better prices. Colleen Barton found a solution to the uncontrolled growth occurring in her company. Her oil drilling consulting and software development venture, GeoMechanics, faced this dilemma. Strategically the company planned to use its low-margin consulting to market its high-margin software. Unfortunately, customers were demanding more and more consulting from her employees, which took time away from developing and marketing the software products. To keep the company focused on technology with controlled growth, she decided to license the technology. One of her competitors who also sells equipment, now markets her software for a licensing fee, and the two firms split revenues on consulting services. For Colleen and her company, this was a good way to expand sales without adding employees, who were difficult to find; it also eliminated investing in new facilities to meet demand.

Pearce Jones, founder and president of Design Edge, found a different solution to controlling growth. His company simply stopped all growth for one year. The company realized that if it did not control its growth, more serious problems were likely to occur. At this time, the company had quadrupled the number of employees and had invested in a new building. Even though each new employee was contributing an increase of $150,000 in sales, the margins were low. Having the additional debt from the new facility and the additional costs for employees, the decision was made to cease hiring, deactivate marketing and sales, refuse any new business, and basically focus on its existing customers. Although Pearce Jones admits this decision was emotionally painful, it led to dramatic changes in the company as profits actually doubled and no employee turnover was experienced.

These three examples indicate different ways for entrepreneurs to manage growth rather than not growing or allowing growth to manage them. This chapter will focus on the entrepreneurial problem of how to successfully grow a venture by focusing on the typical life cycle of a venture, problems involved in growth, entrepreneurial skills enabling growth, financial and organizational strategies for growth, information planning and control, key decisions enabling growth, and characteristics of fast-growth firms.

LIFE CYCLE OF A VENTURE

Figure 10-1 illustrates the typical growth cycle of a new venture. In the first few years of a new venture's existence revenues are relatively small with little growth. This initial phase typically lasts for several years, although it will vary significantly by industry. In the next phase, which typically lasts for several more years, revenues begin to grow at an increasing rate. Then the venture reaches a more balanced phase when revenues and growth stabilize. What occurs after this stage depends on the firm's ability to rejuvenate sales and begin another growth cycle. At this stage the decision in a highly competitive market may be to maintain and protect market share with little or no growth. It is also possible that revenues may even decrease during this stage as the demand for the product declines due to substitute products or changes in consumers' needs. The entrepreneur may choose to control costs and harvest the business or look for new products or strategies to revitalize the growth of the enterprise.

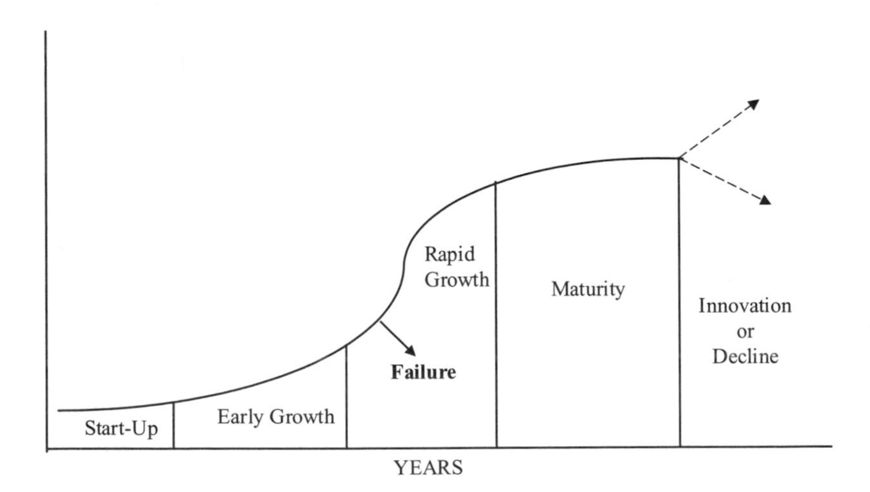

Figure 10-1. Growth cycle of a venture.

Not all new ventures enter the rapid growth phase. Many will continue to exist at some satisfying level of sales with little or no growth. These enterprises, typically proprietorships or partnerships, are home-based, family-owned service (particularly personal services) or craft businesses. For example, a self-employed consultant may be satisfied working alone and serving a client base without any rapid growth. This entrepreneur's revenue base is limited to his or her time available due to the decision not to add more people to the business. This same entrepreneur could instead see an opportunity for growth and hire new people and expand the business into new market segments. In each instance the decision to grow is dictated by the entrepreneur's interest in conjunction with the response of the market to the venture's product or service.

In the period of the Internet craze, Internet start-ups had a different growth cycle. Amazon.com exhibited rapid growth in the first years of existence and continued with double growth over its first 5 years. In 2000 sales jumped to $2.7 billion from $1.4 billion in 1999 continuing its rise to be one of the fastest growing Internet companies in the world. Other Internet companies such as eBay and Yahoo also are representative of this distinctive growth pattern.

However, what happened to many of these Internet firms is what often happens in this rapid growth phase of a venture—failure (see Figure 10-1). Entrepreneurs who do not understand growth and how to control and manage it usually run into problems, which can be serious enough to cause failure. This rapid growth period is only preceded by the start-up period in the number of venture failures. Driven by the need for creativity and growth, the entrepreneur forgets about focusing on and servicing the customer and the quality of the product deteriorates and cost overruns occur. The biggest problem, according to A. Malachi Mixon III, president and CEO of Invacare, who successfully grew his company into the leader in home health-care products, is that "entrepreneurs forget to build a solid infrastructure to support and carry out the growth desired."

Too often the entrepreneur forgets the basic axiom in every business: the only constant is change. Every entrepreneur needs to understand what it takes to grow his or her venture and then decide whether this is the desired strategy. If the choice is growth, then the entrepreneur needs to understand the important management skills and strategies necessary to successfully meet the growth challenge.

GROWTH PROBLEMS

Entrepreneurs often face the problem in their new venture's life known as "hitting the growth wall," where operations reach out-of-control proportions, cash runs out, and key employees leave for more stable jobs. For example, James L. Bildner, the founder of J. Bildner & Sons Inc., a specialty food business, had his company reach a point where he ran out of cash, found employees leaving, and operations becoming unmanageable. After achieving sales of $48 million with more than 20 retail units and having a public offering that fueled rapid growth, the company "hit the wall." With the symptoms described above, the company began to incur large profit losses, inventory control problems, and loss of loyal customers. Too many new locations, ineffective new products, new people, lack of capital, and lack of controls made everything worse.

Typically ventures that are facing this situation hope that future performance will carry them through the difficult times. This hope rests on an unrealistic anticipation of a new contract, the new product that can inject new sales, or the unique sales plan that will turn things around. The reality of these unlikely scenarios is clear to everyone but the entrepreneur, who continues to expect better performance. The tragedy is that the result is usually disastrous. One way to survive this situation is to avoid it altogether by being prepared to manage growth with effective management skills and controls.

Bildner survived hitting the wall by conducting focus groups to learn more about the problems. Employees were included in the assessment and were assured that with good planning the company would survive. Today the company is significantly scaled down, with a small presence in the Boston market, and has survived "hitting the wall" for more than 7 years.

ENTREPRENEURIAL SKILLS FOR GROWTH

During the growth stage of a venture the entrepreneur will need to adopt important management skills. These management skills and strategies in such areas as record keeping and financial control, inventory control, human resources, marketing, and planning are critical to achieving long-term success.

Record Keeping and Financial Control

Maintaining good records and financial controls over such activities as cash flow, inventory, receivables, customer data, and costs need to be a priority of every growing venture. In order to support this effort it is helpful to consider using a software package to enhance the flow of this needed information.

With a growing venture it is sometimes necessary to enlist the external support and services of an accountant or consultant to provide record keeping and financial control. These external service firms can also help train employees using the latest and most appropriate technology that can meet the needs of the venture.

Customer information should be retained in a database and with each customer being labeled as active or inactive. In addition, information on a contact person, telephone number, address, as well as important data on the amount of units and dollars of business transacted by each account should be maintained. New accounts should also be designated for follow-up, such as welcoming customers and providing them with important information about the company and its products and services.

A good example of the importance of customer information to a growth venture involved an engineering firm that was having difficulty communicating from one engineer to another either on-site or in the office. Requests or complaints conveyed to the on-site engineer were not communicated to the home office until the engineer returned. When clients called the home office, they found that the request or complaint had not been forwarded to other engineers. To resolve this problem a manual system was first employed.

Each on-site engineer maintained a logbook in which notes such as any client requests or complaints were recorded. These notes would then be faxed daily to the home office and kept in a client folder. When a client spoke to someone at the home office there would be a file containing all the important information about the client and project. This manual system would then be upgraded using e-mail or laptop computers, which would contain software, such as Maximizer, to maintain customer information using on-line technology.

Inventory Control

During the growth of a new venture, the management of inventory is an important cost control and customer service activity that needs to be carefully monitored. Too much inventory can be a drain on cash flow since manufacturing, transportation, and storage costs are paid by the venture. On the other hand, too little inventory can also cost the venture in lost sales, or it can create unhappy customers who may choose another firm if their needs are not efficiently met.

Effective supply-chain management among producers, wholesalers, and retailers can enable effective communication between the company and channel members. Linking the needs of a retailer to the wholesaler and producer allows for fast order entry and response by the entrepreneurial firm.

For example, in the grocery and pharmaceutical industries, supply-chain members work together to manage demand, distribution, and marketing such that minimum inventory levels are necessary to meet consumer needs. Computerized checkout machines are usually part of these systems enabling linked members to anticipate inventory needs before stockouts occur.

Transportation mode selection can also be important in inventory management. Some transportation modes, such as the use of air, are very expensive. Rail and truck are the most frequently used sources of transportation, when a next-day delivery for a customer is not necessary. Careful management of inventory through a computerized system and by working with customers and other channel members can minimize these transportation costs.

Human Resources

Often the new venture does not have the luxury of a human resource manager or department that can interview, hire, and evaluate employees. Most of these decisions will be the responsibility of the entrepreneur and perhaps one or two other key employees as the new venture grows. As the firm grows, there is almost always a need to hire new employees. Procedures for interviewing, hiring, evaluating, and preparing job descriptions for new employees need to be established.

One of the most difficult decisions for an entrepreneur involves laying off employees. Having an employee evaluation process is important when letting an employee go. Employees should be given feedback on a regular basis, and any problems should be identified, with a proposed solution agreeable to both the employee and the entrepreneur.

Marketing Skills

Marketing skills in the growth stage of a new venture are also critical to a venture's continued success. As the company grows, it will need to develop new products and services to maintain its distinctiveness in a competitive market. This should be an ongoing process based on information regarding changing customer needs and competitive strategies. This information can be obtained formally using surveys or focus groups, or informally by direct contact with customers by the entrepreneur or his or her sales force. Some entrepreneurs have found that occasional travel with the sales force to key accounts can be very revealing and often lead to ideas for new products.

In a small growing entrepreneurial venture, it is difficult to engage in some of the more formal procedures for developing new products because of the lack of people and financial resources. Universities, however, frequently offer the opportunity for a small business to participate as part of a student project in a marketing research class at little or no cost. The Internet also can be a good resource to provide market information.

The marketing plan should be prepared on an annual basis. The marketing plan should designate goals and objectives, and outline action programs for the next year. Key employees, customers, and channel members should be used in the preparation and implementation of this plan.

Strategic Planning Skills

To grow the venture successfully, it is also important for the entrepreneur to plan both for the short term and the long term. Planning is a continual process, particularly in a rapidly changing, hypercompetitive environment. Strategic or long-range planning begins with a reiteration of the mission statement of the venture and ends with feedback and control.

Hamish Hafter, CEO of Mishi Apparel, found that distributing a questionnaire to each of the employees of his firm was a meaningful way to understand a particular situation. Questions were asked about what the employees thought was working well in the department or what aspects needed change. Reponses were collected, summarized, and distributed to help launch the strategic planning process. By guaranteeing anonymity, this is an effective method for the entrepreneur to learn more about internal and external issues shared by everyone. Further meetings can then be used to prepare the situation analysis and begin the next step in the strategic planning process.

FINANCIAL STRATEGIES FOR GROWTH

While it is the primary focus of Chapter 12, it is important to stress here the importance of managing the cash flow of a business. This does not change during the growth stage but, in fact, becomes even more critical since it is often difficult to maintain close scrutiny of where cash is going. In particular the entrepreneur will need to determine how much cash will be needed to accommodate the rapid sales growth.

INFORMATION PLANNING AND CONTROL

It is very important throughout the life of the venture that management and financial controls to evaluate cash flows, profits, costs, inventory, and sales are developed and used. These control systems are particularly important during the growth stage of a venture. In addition to financial and management control, the entrepreneur needs to establish information/customer service tracking systems and controls.

Customer Service/Satisfaction Tracking

Entrepreneurs need to pay significant attention to the customers and establish processes that track and monitor *customer service and satisfaction.* Unlike financial, inventory, and sales controls, the monitoring of customer satisfaction involves more qualitative measures that can provide early warnings to the entrepreneur of impending customer problems. These problems can affect financial results as well as sales revenue, and thus constant evaluation and monitoring are important. Monitoring and tracking customer satisfaction can be performed in a number of ways that are not costly to the entrepreneur or the new venture.

All complaints, suggestions, and comments that come from customers either orally or in writing need to be recorded and assessed on a regular basis. These should be kept in a folder and summarized by someone on staff. The entrepreneur should plan regular meetings to discuss with his or her staff why the complaints are occurring and the solutions needed to resolve any problems. While a random complaint may not need any special attention, since it is difficult to be able to always please every customer, the entrepreneur may find that a random or isolated complaint is an impending problem or is embedded in other related problems.

KEY DECISIONS FOR GROWTH

There are some key decisions that entrepreneurs make that enable growth to occur, which if not made in a timely fashion, can negatively affect the growth and performance of the venture. These decisions tend to occur most frequently in the following areas: increasing human resources, increasing raw material sources and production capacity, adding distribution channels, raising additional financing, and forming strategic alliances.

Increasing Human Resources

One of the most critical decisions in growing a new venture is the timing of adding new employees. This is particularly important at the management level as the new venture cannot grow without new managers, and yet the cost of the additional manager is usually not initially offset by an additional increase in sales and/or profits to the firm. Adding higher-level managers is perhaps the most difficult challenge for an entrepreneur as not only does the addition increase payroll costs but it also requires a change in the entrepreneur's management style. Such a difficult decision was made by Tom Kitchin, president and CEO of Jameson Inns, Inc. Jameson Inns, headquartered in Atlanta, develops and owns limited-service hotel properties (inns) in the southwestern United States under the trademark "The Jameson Inn." The corporation also owns full-service hotels in the Midwestern United States under the trademark "Signature Inn." The company was growing strongly by opening inns in communities having a strong and growing industrial or commercial base, targeting business travelers. As the number of inns kept increasing it became apparent that they could no longer be managed by one individual from the corporate office but instead would need to be grouped together based on geographic location under regional managers.

The addition of these new regional managers by Tom Kitchin allowed the company to continue to grow, with new inns being developed in strategic locations. Today the company has 98 Jameson Inns in Alabama, Florida, Georgia, Kentucky, Louisiana, Mississippi, North Carolina, South Carolina, Tennessee, and Virginia, as well as 26 Signature Inns in Indiana, Illinois, Iowa, Kentucky, Ohio, and Tennessee.

Increasing Production Capacity

Another problem facing entrepreneurs is when to increase production and therefore increase the supply of raw materials. This was a problem facing Dale Morris, president and CEO of Nature Brothers, Inc., a start-up company introducing a new seasoning salt mix. The product was a low-salt seasoning mix, based on a nutritive yeast extract that could be used as a salt substitute. While his kitchen-scale operation produced enough to support the sales effort of the Ladies Mission Society of his church as a fund-raising effort, if he wanted to take advantage of these truly marketable products, new production capabilities would have to be developed at some significant costs. Dale Morris decided to move ahead and began aggressively marketing his seasoning mix, Nature Brothers Seasoning Mix, through grocery stores in Oklahoma and Texas, based on the production from newly acquired computer-controlled filling and seaming equipment in a new company plant located in Oklahoma.

Adding Distribution Channels

A third problem in growing a company, particularly one producing consumer goods, is the timing of adding additional distribution channels. Not only does it require time and usually money in the form of "slotting allowances," but each new distribution channel requires additional inventory as well as establishing a new distribution system for the new channel members. This was the problem confronting Lou Major, president and CEO of Polymer Technology, Inc., the producer of the Boston Lens and the Boston Lens Solutions, in Woburn, Massachusetts. After successfully introducing the Boston Lens and the Boston Lens Solutions in the Toronto, Canada, market area, it soon became clear that a supply-chain network would need to be established so that the Boston Lens Cleaning and Boston Lens Wetting and Soaking Solutions would be available in retail stores throughout Canada. This would then coincide with the introduction of the Boston Lens, the first gas-permeable hard contact lens, to optometrists throughout the country. Lou Major and his associate made the decision to hire a manufacturer representative based in Toronto to sell the solutions throughout Canada by establishing key accounts all over the country.

Raising Additional Finances

One of the most difficult problems in growing a venture is raising the necessary additional money to fund the growth. These funds may take the form of debt or equity, with the entrepreneur having to deal with bank managers, angel investors, venture capitalists, or perhaps investment bankers to access the public equity market. Stephanie Harkness, president and CEO of Pacific Plastics and Engineering, in Soquel, California, funds the growth of her firm by maintaining a strong relationship with her bank. This debt form of financing is particularly important for Stephanie Harkness as she does not want to have an equity partner and still wants to grow her $10 million firm, which produces customized plastic injection molding. She has developed this strong banking relationship by always sending the bank monthly financial statements and allowing the bank to assist her in capital planning. Since a new injection-molding machine costs $100,000, it is important to time the purchase carefully with respect to increased customer demands. This strong relationship, among other things, resulted in Pacific Plastics and Engineering receiving a 50 percent credit line increase from the bank.

Forming Strategic Alliances

A final timely decision for growth is establishing of the right strategic alliance or developing strategic partners. This was the recent solution for Alexander Chuenko, president and CEO of Doka Company, a

Russian entrepreneurial company founded in May 1987 in Zelenograd, a district of Moscow. While the company was growing through its telecommunications and information technologies, biotechnologies, microelectronics and software, machinery and special equipment, and financial operations, a unique opportunity occurred in the form of a new computer game, Total Control, which was available in four languages—Russian, German, French, and English. Lacking any international marketing experience or sales network, Alexander Chuenko decided to market this game and other software products of the company globally by establishing partnerships with such companies as Spectrum HoloByte (United States), Lexicon Software (United States), Bullet Proof Software (Japan), VIF (France), Infogames (France), Sybex Verlas (Germany), ZYX (Germany), Peruzzo Information (Italy), and Scandinavian CD-Rom Publishers (Denmark). Doka supplied each partner with master disks and the license to publish and market the game and other software products in their agreed-upon territory. By working through partners, Alexander Chuenko was able to continue to grow the Doka Company in spite of the turbulent Russian economy and currency.

Similarly, the use of alliances allowed smaller advertising agencies to vie for the business of a prestigious car company—DaimlerChrysler. The Chrysler Group in the United States invited advertising agencies to compete for its multiculture account of masterminding the advertising campaign of Chrysler, Jeep, and Dodge cars and trucks to the urban marketplace, allowing alliances to be a part of the competition. Since few small agencies could meet the terms of the request for proposal (RFP) of the company, alliances of two to four agencies were formed with names such as PASS Urban Powertrain. The five semifinalists in the RFP were all alliances and one of these alliances won the contract of the Chrysler Group.

CHARACTERISTICS OF GROWING VENTURES

Regardless of the type of decisions that affected the growth of the venture, there are several characteristics of fast-growing firms.

First, fast-growing firms have leaders with a clear vision that put employees at the forefront of their decisions. In this aspect, the leader is like a gardener. One does not manufacture a tomato, one grows it. One takes a seed and cultivates it, fertilizes it, adds water to it throughout its development into a plant yielding fruit. Similarly, a leader of a fast-growing company has a vision and shares that vision with his or her employees so that they clearly see and share the vision. Employee can then help operationalize that vision into a successful growing company. Remember, Jesus took a towel and basin and washed feet, and so redefined leadership.

Second, fast-growing companies retain small-company traits such as sharing the focus and being flexible, part of the focus of Chapters 4 and 6. This requires that the company be managed intrapreneurially, and where possible, strategic business units should be established so that smaller groups of employees can work together and share the rewards of successfully managing particular product/market groups. Employee creativity, initiative, and ownership should be strongly encouraged and rewarded. A fast-growing company needs to be very flexible so changes can be made quickly in its hypercompetitive environment. These changes may even involve a complete redirection of the company as occurred in Arnolite Pallet Company in Westport, Indiana. The company, under the direction of the founder and president/CEO Arno Lessheim, had been formed to commercialize a new plastic molded modular cup pallet. However, when the market resisted this new entry, the company changed its product to wooden pallets and successfully competed in the wooden pallet product/market space until the market was ready for the plastic molded pallet, which the company later produced.

Finally, a fast-growing company has a focus on its customers and has a strong belief in customer service. This customer focus and belief in customer service is what led the Magna Lock Company to establish a new method of distribution. The company was producing and selling a new antitheft device that would cut off the gas supply in an automobile when the fixture was positioned in a specific manner. In order to make it very convenient for the consumer, the company developed a procedure to install the device in the parking lot of the customer's workplace or home. Pepsi Cola/Frito Lay so believes in customer focus and service that it has the policy that no store, no matter how small, will be out of stock of its product for more than 24 hours.

By understanding the life cycle of the venture as well as anticipating possible growth problems, the entrepreneur can implement key decisions and strategies that will allow his or her company to grow successfully.

Part III

FINANCE PROBLEMS

11

Raising Capital

PROFILE—RICK SARMIENTO

Rick Sarmiento, president and CEO of White House/Black Market, a retailer of women's apparel in Baltimore, Maryland, started his business in 1989. His retail business of selling fashionable clothing in shades of only black and white continued to expand, reaching 35 stores by 1998 through debt financing. Rick Sarmiento was facing a problem: How could he continue the company's expansion in pace with such a hot retail concept? It was impossible to continue this rapid expansion by increasing the debt obligation of the company, as the company's cash flow was already being squeezed by the present debt burden.

Reluctantly Rick Sarmiento turned to the equity market and obtained $8.6 million of capital infusion from a venture capital firm knowledgeable about retail operations, Phillips-Smith-Machens Venture Partners and its investment partner, Invesco Private Capital, Inc. The venture capital company's principals had successful retail careers and did not micromanage their portfolio companies. They had previously invested in and taken public an impressive list of companies, including CompUSA Inc., Hot Topic Inc., Cheap Tickets, Inc., and PetsMart Inc. From 1998 to present, the venture capital firm has helped Rick Sarmiento and White House/Black Market pay off the large debt burden, remodel existing shops, and open 35 new stores. The venture capital firm provided the company with capital, retailing prowess, and connections to strengthen the company's board and operating capabilities. Important changes were instituted in the company's merchandising and buying procedures, increasing the average sales per square foot of the company's retail space by about 40 percent.

White House/Black Market beat its sales targets every month in 2002 and is approaching $100 million in annual revenues as of the writing of this book. The company's goal is to increase to approximately 100 stores.

As Rick Sarmiento now knows, one of the most difficult problems facing entrepreneurs is raising capital and choosing the correct equity structure. This chapter provides solutions to these problems by discussing debt versus equity financing, use of internal versus external funds, the types of external funds available, the stages in business financing, and bootstrap financing.

DEBT VERSUS EQUITY FINANCING

Two overall types of financing are available to the entrepreneur: debt financing and equity financing. *Debt financing* is a financing method involving an interest-bearing instrument, usually a loan, the payment of which is only indirectly related to the sales and profits of the venture. Typically, debt financing (also called asset-based financing) requires that some asset (such as a car, house, plant, machine, or land) be used as collateral.

Debt financing requires the entrepreneur to pay back the amount of funds borrowed as well as a fee expressed in terms of the interest rate. There can also be an additional fee, sometimes referred to as points, for using or being able to borrow the money depending on the credit standing and assets of the entrepreneur and the business. If the financing is short-term (less than one year), the money usually is used to provide working capital to finance inventory, accounts receivable, or the operation of the business. The funds are typically repaid from the resulting sales and profits during the year. Long-term debt (lasting more than 1 year) frequently is used to purchase some asset such as machinery, land, or a building, with part of the value of the asset (usually around 50 percent of the total value) being used as collateral for the long-term loan. Particularly when interest rates are low, debt (as opposed to equity) financing allows the entrepreneur to retain a larger ownership portion in the venture and have a greater return on equity. The entrepreneur needs to be careful that the debt is not so large that regular interest payments become difficult if not impossible to make.

Equity financing does not require collateral and offers the investor some form of ownership position in the venture. The investor shares in the profits of the venture, as well as any disposition of its assets on a pro rata basis. Key factors favoring the use of one type of financing over another are the availability of funds, the assets of the venture, and the prevailing interest rates. Usually, an entrepreneur raises the capital needed by employing a combination of both debt and equity financing.

USE OF INTERNAL OR EXTERNAL FUNDS

Financing also is available from internal or external funds. The type of funds most frequently employed are internally generated funds. Internally generated funds can come from several sources within the company—profits, sale of assets, reduction in working capital, extended payment terms, and accounts receivable. In every new venture, the start-up years usually involve plowing all or a significant part of the profits back into the venture. The needed funds sometimes can be obtained by selling little-used assets. Assets, whenever possible, should be on a rental basis (preferably on a lease with an option to buy), not on an ownership basis, as long as there is not a high level of inflation and the rental terms are favorable with low interest rates. This will help the entrepreneur to conserve cash, a practice that is particularly critical during the start-up phase of the company's operation, the focus of Chapter 12.

The other general source of funds is external to the venture. Alternative sources of external financing need to be evaluated on three bases—the length of time the funds are available, the costs

Table 11-1. Alternative sources of financing.

Source of Financing	Length of Time		Cost			Control	
	Short-term	Long-term	Fixed Rate Debt	Floating Rate Debt	Equity	Covenants	Voting Rights
Self		X			X	X	X
Family and friends	X	X	X	X	X	X	X
Suppliers and trade credit	X						
Commercial banks	X		X	X		X	
Government programs		X					
Private equity placements		X			X	X	X
Public equity offerings		X			X		X
Angel financing		X			X	X	X
Venture capital financing		X			X	X	X

involved, and the amount of company control lost. In selecting the best source of funds, each of the sources indicated in Table 11-1 needs to be evaluated along these three dimensions.

TYPES OF EXTERNAL FUNDS

Examples of the more frequently used sources of funds include self, family and friends, commercial banks, Small Business Administration (SBA) loans, R&D limited partnerships, government grants, and private placement. These are shown in Table 11-1 and are further discussed below.

Personal Funds

Few, if any, new ventures are started without the personal funds of the entrepreneur. Not only are these the least expensive funds in terms of cost and control, but they are also absolutely essential in attracting any additional outside funding, particularly from banks, private investors, and venture capitalists. These outside providers of capital feel that the entrepreneur may not be sufficiently committed to the venture if he or she does not have personal money invested. As one venture capitalist succinctly said, "I want the entrepreneurs so financially committed that when the going gets tough, they will work through the problems and not throw the keys to the company on my desk."

This level of commitment is reflected in the percentage of total assets available to the entrepreneur that he or she has committed, not necessarily only the amount of money committed. An outside investor wants an entrepreneur to have committed all available assets, an indicator that he or she truly believes in the venture and will work all hours necessary to make success possible. Whether this is $1,000, $100,000, or $250,000 depends on the assets of the entrepreneur. One should always remember that it is not simply the amount, but rather the fact that all available monies are committed, that makes outside investors feel comfortable with the risk and commitment of the entrepreneur and therefore willing to invest.

Family and Friends

After the entrepreneur, family and friends are the next most common source of capital for a new venture. Family members and friends usually invest due to their relationship with the entrepreneur. This helps overcome one portion of uncertainty felt by impersonal investors—familiarity with the entrepreneur. Family and friends are the major providers of equity funding for new ventures, reflecting in part the small amount of capital needed for most new ventures. Even though it is relatively easy to obtain money from family and friends, like all sources of capital, it has its positive and negative aspects. Even though the amount of money provided may be small, if it is in the form of equity financing, the family member or friend then has an ownership position in the venture and all corresponding rights and privileges of that position. This may make them feel they have a direct input into the operations of the venture, which may have a negative impact on employees, facilities, sales, or profits. Although this possibility must be guarded against as much as possible by having a signed legal agreement in place, most of the time family and friends are not problem investors and in fact are more patient than other investors.

In order to avoid problems in the future, the entrepreneur should present both the positive and negative aspects as well as the nature of the risks of the investment opportunity to any investing family and friends. One thing that helps minimize possible difficulties is to establish a formal business arrangement regarding the investments. Any loans or investments from family or friends should be treated in the same businesslike manner that the financing would be from an impersonal outside investor. Any loan should specify the rate of interest and the proposed repayment schedule of interest and principal. The timing of any future dividends or payout of any equity investment should be specified. If the family or friend is treated the same as any investor, potential future conflicts can be avoided. It is amazing how short memories become when money is involved. Each transaction should have a signed legal agreement specifying all the conditions of the deal. All the details of the financing must be agreed upon before the money is put into the venture. Such things as the amount of money involved, the terms of the money, the rights and responsibilities of the investor, and what happens if the business fails must all be agreed upon and written down.

Finally, the entrepreneur should carefully consider the impact of the investment on the family member or friend before it is accepted. Particular concern should be paid to any hardships that might result should the business fail. Each family member or friend should be investing in the venture because they think it is a good investment, not because they feel obligated to the entrepreneur because of personal and/or family relationships.

Commercial Banks

Commercial banks are the major source of short-term funds for the entrepreneur when collateral is available. The funds provided are in the form of debt financing, and as such require some tangible guarantee or collateral—some asset with value. This collateral can be in the form of business assets (land, equipment, or the building of the venture), personal assets (the entrepreneur's house, car, land, stock, or bonds), or the assets of the cosigner of the note.

Types of Bank Loans

There are several types of bank loans available. To ensure repayment, these loans are based on the assets or the cash flow of the venture. The asset base for loans usually is accounts receivable, inventory, equipment, or real estate.

The other type of debt financing frequently provided by commercial banks and other financial institutions is cash-flow financing. These conventional bank loans include lines of credit, installment loans, straight commercial loans, long-term loans, and character loans. Lines of credit financing are perhaps the form of cash-flow financing most frequently used by entrepreneurs. In arranging for a line of credit to be used as needed, the company pays a "commitment fee" to ensure that the commercial bank will make the loan when requested and then pays interest on any outstanding funds borrowed from the bank. Frequently, the loan must be repaid or reduced to a certain agreed-upon level on a periodic basis.

When the business itself does not have the assets to support a loan, the entrepreneur may need a character (personal) loan. These loans frequently must have the assets of the entrepreneur or another individual pledged as collateral, or the loan cosigned by another individual. Assets that are frequently pledged include homes, land, stocks, and bonds. One entrepreneur's father pledged a $50,000 certificate of deposit as collateral for his son's $40,000 loan. In extremely rare instances, the entrepreneur can obtain money on an unsecured basis for a short time when a high credit standing has been established.

Bank Lending Decisions

One problem for the entrepreneur is determining how to successfully secure a loan from the bank. Banks are generally cautious in lending money, particularly to new ventures, since they do not want to incur losses through bad loans. Regardless of geographic location, commercial loan decisions are made only after the loan officer and loan committee do a careful review of the borrower and the financial track record of the business and/or its business plan. These decisions are based on both quantifiable information and subjective judgments.

The bank lending decisions are made according to the five Cs of lending—Character, Capacity, Capital, Collateral, and Conditions. Past financial statements (balance sheets and income statements) are reviewed in terms of key profitability and credit ratios, inventory turnover, aging of accounts receivable, the amount of entrepreneur's capital invested, and commitment to the business. Future projections on market size, sales, and profitability also are evaluated to determine the ability of the firm to repay the loan. Several questions usually are raised regarding this ability. Does the entrepreneur expect to be carried by the loan for an extended period of time? If problems occur, is the entrepreneur committed enough to spend the effort necessary to make the business a success? Does the business have a unique differential advantage in a growth market? What are the downside risks? Is there protection (such as life insurance on key personnel and insurance on the plant and equipment) against disasters?

Although the answers to these questions and the analysis of the company's records allow the loan officer to assess the quantitative aspects of the loan decision, the intuitive factors, particularly character and capacity, also are taken into account. This part of the loan decision—the gut feeling—is the most difficult part of the decision to assess. The entrepreneur must present his or her capabilities and the prospects for the company in a way that elicits a positive response from the lender. This intuitive part of the loan decision becomes even more important when there is little or no track record, limited experience in financial management, a nonproprietary product or service (one not protected by a patent or license), or few assets available.

Some concerns of the loan officer and loan committee can be eliminated by providing a good loan application. While the specific loan application format of each bank differs to some extent, generally the application format is a mini business plan that consists of an executive summary, business description, owner/manager profiles, business projections, financial statements, amount and use of the loan, and repayment schedule. Having a well-formulated complete business plan is a plus. This information provides the loan officer and loan committee insight into the creditworthiness of the individual and the venture as well as the ability of the venture to make enough sales and profit to repay the loan with the interest. The entrepreneur should valuate several alternative lending institutions, select the one that has had positive loan experience in the particular industry area, set up an appointment, and then carefully present the case for the loan to the loan officer. Presenting a positive business image and following the established protocol are helpful in obtaining a loan from a commercial bank.

Generally, the entrepreneur should borrow the maximum amount that can be repaid as long as the prevailing interest rates and the terms, conditions, and restrictions of the loan are satisfactory. It is essential that the venture generate enough cash flow to repay the interest and principal on the loan in a timely manner. The entrepreneur should evaluate the track record and lending procedures of several banks in order to secure the money needed on the most favorable terms available. This "bank shopping procedure" will help obtain the needed funds at the most favorable rates. As one entrepreneur, A. Malachi Mixon III, chairman and CEO of Invacare, so succinctly stated: "You need to make sure your bank knows you and your company well. Then they are available when you need a loan. Treat the bank as a customer, not a supplier."

Small Business Administration Loans

Frequently, an entrepreneur is missing the necessary track record, assets, or some other ingredient to obtain a commercial bank loan. When the entrepreneur is unable to secure a regular commercial bank loan, an alternative is a Small Business Administration (SBA) Guaranty Loan. In this loan, the SBA guarantees that 80 percent of the amount loaned to the entrepreneur's business will be repaid by the SBA if the entrepreneurial venture cannot make payment. This guarantee allows the bank to make a loan that has a higher risk than loans it would otherwise make. The process for securing such a loan is outlined in Table 11-2. This procedure is the same as the one used for securing a regular loan, except there are government forms and

Table 11-2. Required materials for SBA loans.

1. Application for Loan: SBA form 4, 4I
2. Statement of Personal History: SBA form 912
3. Personal Financial Statement: SBA form 413
4. Detailed, signed Balance Sheet and Profit and Loss Statements current (within 90 days of application) and last three (3) fiscal years Supplementary Schedules required on Current Financial Statements.
5. Detailed one (1) year projection of Income & Finances (please attach written explanation as to how you expect to achieve same).
6. A list of names and addresses of any subsidiaries and affiliates, including concerns in which the applicant holds a controlling (but not necessarily a majority) interest and other concerns that may be affiliated by stock ownership, franchise, proposed merger or otherwise with the applicant.
7. Certificate of Doing Business (if a corporation, stamp corporate seals on SBA form 4 section 12).
8. By Law, the Agency may not guarantee a loan if a business can obtain funds on reasonable terms from a bank or other private source. A borrower therefore must first seek private financing. A company must be independently owned and operated, not dominant in its field and must meet certain standards of size in terms of employees or annual receipts. Loans cannot be made to speculative businesses, newspapers, or businesses engaged in gambling. Applicants for loans must also agree to comply with SBA regulation that there will be no discrimination in employment or services to the public, based on race, color, religion, national origin, sex or marital status.
9. Signed Business Federal Income Tax Returns for previous three (3) years.
10. Signed Personal Federal Income Tax Returns of principals for previous three (3) years.
11. Personal Resume including business experience of each principal.
12. Brief history of the business and its problems: Include an explanation of why the SBA loan is needed and how it will help the business.
13. Copy of Business Lease (or note from landlord giving terms of proposed lease).

Source: Small Business Administration—www.sba.gov/gopher/Financial-Assistance/rego.txt.

documentation required. Usually, some banks will specialize in these types of loans and are better able to assist the entrepreneur in completing the appropriate forms correctly. This minimizes the time involved in the government's processing and approving (or dis- approving) the loan. These banks are often listed annually in *Inc.* magazine. If an SBA Guaranty Loan is granted, additional reporting practices are required beyond those that exist with a conventional bank loan.

Government Grants

The entrepreneur sometimes can obtain federal grant money to develop and launch an innovative idea. A program of particular interest designed for the small business is the Small Business Innovation Development Act. The act requires that all federal agencies with R&D budgets in excess of $100 million award a portion of their R&D funds to small businesses through the Small Business Innovation Research Program (SBIR) grants program.

Eleven federal agencies are involved in the program, including the Department of Defense, the Department of Energy, and the National Science Foundation. Each agency develops R&D topics and publishes solicitations describing the R&D topic it will fund. Small businesses submit proposals directly to each agency using the required format, which is somewhat standardized, regardless of the agency. Each agency, using its established evaluation criteria, evaluates each proposal on a competitive basis and makes awards through a contract, grant, or cooperative agreement.

Applying for an SBIR grant is a straightforward procedure. The participating government agencies publish solicitations describing the areas of research they will fund. Each of these annual solicitations contains documentation on the agency's R&D objectives, proposal format, due dates, deadlines, and selection and evaluation criteria.

Private Placement/Business Angels

Another source of funds for the entrepreneur are private investors, often called *business angels*. These wealthy individuals frequently use advisors such as accountants, technical experts, financial planners, or lawyers, in making their investment decisions.

An angel usually takes an equity position in the entrepreneur's company and can influence the nature and direction of the business to some extent. The angel may even be involved to some degree in the operation of the business. The degree of involvement in the direction or the day-to-day operations of the venture is an important point for the entrepreneur to consider in selecting an investor. Some investors want to be actively involved in the business, while others desire at least an advisory role in the direction and operation of the venture.

A formalized approach for obtaining funds from private investors is through a private offering. These private sophisticated investors need access to material information about the company and its management. What constitutes material information? Who is a sophisticated investor? How many is a limited number? Answers to these questions are provided in Regulation D and can be obtained from the Securities and Exchange Commission (SEC).

Another option to a more formalized private placement is obtaining money from one or more business angels in the informal risk-capital market, the most misunderstood and inefficient type of risk capital. The market consists of a virtually invisible group of wealthy investors who are looking for equity-type investment opportunities in a wide variety of entrepreneurial ventures. Typically investing anywhere from $10,000 to $500,000, these angels provide the funds needed in all stages of financing, but particularly in start-up (first-stage) financing. Firms funded from the informal risk-capital market frequently raise second- and third-round financing from professional venture-capital firms or the public-equity market.

Despite being misunderstood by, and virtually inaccessible to, many entrepreneurs, the informal investment market contains the largest single pool of risk capital in the United States of about $80 billion.

The size and number of these angel investors have increased dramatically, due in part to the rapid accumulation of wealth in various sectors of the economy. One study found that each of 1.3 million

U.S. families had a net worth of over $1 million. These families, representing about 2 percent of the population, accumulated most of their wealth from earnings, not inheritance, and invested over $151 billion in nonpublic businesses in which they have no management interest. Each year, over 100,000 individual investors finance between 30,000 and 50,000 firms, with a total dollar investment of between $7 billion and $10 billion. Given their investment capability, it is important to know the characteristics of these angels.

These informal investors, or business angels, tend to be well educated; many have graduate degrees. Although they will finance firms anywhere in the United States (and a few in other parts of the world), most of the firms that receive funding are within one day's travel. Business angels tend to make one to two deals each year, with individual firm investments ranging from $10,000 to $500,000, with the average being $175,000. If the opportunity is right, angels might even invest from $500,000 to $1 million. In some cases, angels will join with other angels, usually from a common circle of friends, to finance larger deals.

Where do these angel investors generally find their deals? Deals are found through referrals by business associates, friends, active personal research, investment bankers, accountants, professors, and business brokers. However, even though these *referral sources* provide some deals, most angel investors are not satisfied with the number and type of investment referrals.

Venture Capital

Venture capital is one of the least understood areas in entrepreneurship. It is best to view venture capital broadly as a professionally managed pool of equity capital. The investments are in early-stage deals as well as second- and third-stage deals and leveraged buyouts. In each investment, the venture capitalist takes an *equity participation* through stock, warrants, and/or convertible securities and has an active involvement in the monitoring of each portfolio company bringing investment, financial planning, and business skills to the firm. There are five basic types of venture capital firms, as indicated in Figure 11-1.

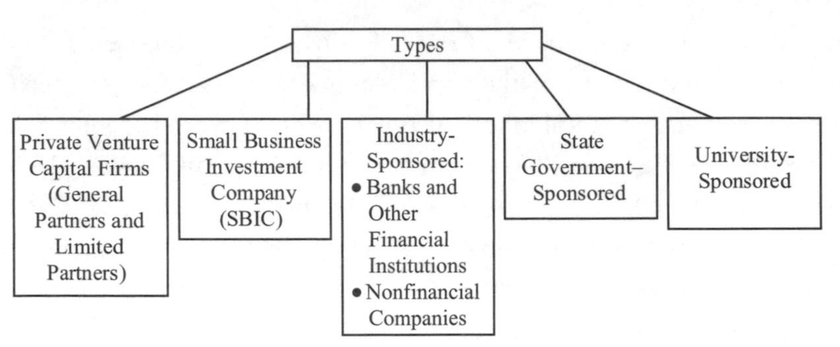

Figure 11-1. Types of venture capital firms.

The Small Business Investment Company Act of 1958, married private capital with government funds to be used by professionally managed small business investment companies (SBICs) to infuse capital into start-up and growing small businesses. With the tax advantages, government funds for leverage, and a private capital company, SBICs were the start of the now formal venture capital industry. There are approximately 360 SBICs operating today, of which 130 are minority small business investment companies (MESBICs), funding minority enterprises.

During the late 1960s, *private venture capital firms* emerged. These were usually formed as limited partnerships, with the venture capital company acting as the general partner receiving a management fee and a percentage of the profits earned on a deal. The limited partners, who supplied the funding, were frequently institutional investors such as insurance companies, endowment funds, bank trust departments, pension funds, and wealthy individuals and families. There are about 980 venture capital establishments in the United States today.

In response to the need for economic development, a fourth type of venture capital firm has emerged in the form of the *state-sponsored venture capital fund.* These state-sponsored funds have a variety of formats. While the size, investment focus, and industry orientation vary from state to state, each fund typically is required to invest a certain percentage of its capital in the particular state. Generally, the funds are professionally managed by the private sector, outside the bureaucracy and political processes of the state.

The final two types of venture capital firms are industry-sponsored and university-sponsored (Figure 11-1). Industry-sponsored venture capital firms are of two types—those of banks and other financial institutions and those of nonfinancial companies. Most major banks and other financial institutions have their own venture capital divisions. Banks such as Citigroup, Key Bank, First National Bank, and First Chicago Bank all have a venture capital division that operates like a private venture capital firm in terms of investment strategy and process. If the venture capital division of a bank invests in a company, then the banking division is prohibited from being financially involved with that company. The other type of industry-sponsored venture capital firms are in nonfinancial companies such as General Motors, Ford, Occidental Petroleum, Johnson and Johnson, 3M, Monsanto, and Eli Lilly. These venture capital divisions of major firms invest only in the technology and industry area of the financing company, both internally and externally. If an entrepreneur has some technology in energy, then an energy company such as Occidental Petroleum could be a source of financing. Usually, these companies are interested in investing in the state of technology of their industry and find investing in external companies a successful method for augmenting their own internal research.

The final type of venture capital firm, university-sponsored, is the newest form of venture capital. Universities such as Case University, Babson College, Columbia University, and Stanford University have established venture capital funds located on their campus, usually in the business school, to invest not only in the technology of the university but in technologies in the region as well. Usually these funds are smaller than the typical venture capital firm and tend to focus on early-stage financing.

To be in a position to secure the funds needed, an entrepreneur must understand the philosophy and objectives of a venture capital firm and its *decision process.* The objective of any type of venture capital firm is to generate long-term capital appreciation through debt and equity investments. To achieve this objective, the venture capitalist is willing to make any changes or modifications necessary in the business investment. Since the objective of the entrepreneur is the survival of the business, the objectives of the two can be at odds, particularly when problems occur.

The venture capitalist does not necessarily seek control of a company, but would rather have the start-up firm and the entrepreneur at the most risk. The venture capitalist usually will want at least one seat on the board of directors. Once the decision to invest is made, the venture capitalist will do anything necessary to support the management team so that the business and the investment prosper. Whereas the venture capitalist expects to provide guidance as a member of the board of directors, the management team is expected to direct and run the daily operations of the company. A venture capitalist will support the management team with investment dollars, financial skills, planning, and expertise in any area needed.

Since the venture capitalist provides long-term investment (typically 5 to 7 years or more), it is important that there be mutual trust and understanding between the entrepreneur and the venture capitalist. There should be no surprises in the firm's performance. Both good and bad news should be shared, with the objective of taking the necessary action to allow the company to grow and develop in the long run. The venture capitalist should be available to the entrepreneur to discuss problems and develop strategic plans.

Since venture capitalists receive many more plans than they are capable of funding, many plans are screened out as soon as possible. They tend to focus more time and effort on those plans that are referred. One venture capital group said that 80 percent of their investments over the last 5 years were in referred companies. Consequently, it is well worth the entrepreneur's time to seek out a personal introduction to the venture capitalist. Typically this referral can be through an executive of a portfolio company, an accountant, lawyer, banker, or business school professor.

The entrepreneur should be aware of some basic rules of thumb in obtaining funding from a venture capital firm. First, great care should be taken in selecting the right venture capitalist to approach. Venture capitalists tend to specialize in certain industries and rarely will invest in a business outside these areas, regardless of the merits of the business proposal and plan. Second, recognize that venture capitalists know each other, particularly in a specific region of the country. When a large amount of money is involved, often they will invest in the deal together, with one venture capital firm taking the lead. Since this degree of familiarity is present, a venture capital firm probably will find out if others have seen your business plan. Do not shop among venture capitalists, as even a good business plan can quickly become "shopworn." Third, when meeting the venture capitalist, particularly for the first time, bring only one or two key members of the management team. A venture capitalist is investing in you and your management team and its track record, not in outside consultants and experts. Any experts can be called in as needed.

Finally, be sure to develop a succinct, well-thought-out oral presentation. This should cover the company's business, the uniqueness of the product or service, the prospects for growth, the major factors behind achieving the sales and profits indicated, the backgrounds and track records of the key managers, the amount of financing required, and the returns anticipated. This first presentation is critical, as is indicated in the comment of one venture capitalist: "I need to sense a competency, a capability, a chemistry within the first half-hour of our initial meeting. The entrepreneur needs to look me in the eye and present his or story clearly and logically. If a chemistry does not start to develop, I start looking for reasons not to do the deal."

Going Public

Going public occurs when the entrepreneur and other equity owners of the venture offer for sale and sell some part of the company to the public through a registration statement filed with the Securities and Exchange Commission (SEC) pursuant to the Securities Act of 1933. The resulting capital infusion to the company from the increased number of stockholders and outstanding shares of stock provide the company with financial resources and a relatively liquid investment forum. Consequently, the company will have greater access to capital markets in the future and a more objective picture of the public's perception of the value of the business. However, given the reporting requirements, the increased number of stockholders, and the costs involved, the entrepreneur must carefully evaluate the advantages and disadvantages of going public before initiating the process.

Two major problems of going public are exposure and the potential loss of control that can occur in a publicly traded company. To stay on the cutting edge of technology, companies frequently need to sacrifice short-term profits for long-term innovation. This can require reinvesting in technology that, in itself, may not produce any bottom-line results, particularly in the short run. Making long-term decisions can be difficult in publicly traded companies where sales/profit evaluations indicate the capability of management via stock values. When enough shares are sold to the public, the company can lose control of decision making, which can even result in the company being acquired through an unfriendly tender offer.

INVESTING CRITERIA AND FINANCING STAGES

Equity investors expect a company to satisfy three general criteria before investing in the venture. First, the company must have a strong management team that consists of individuals with solid experience and backgrounds, a strong commitment to the company, capabilities in their specific areas of expertise, the ability to meet challenges, and the flexibility to scramble wherever necessary. An investor would rather invest in a first-rate management team and a second-rate product than the reverse. The commitment of the management team should be reflected in dollars invested in the company. Although the amount of the investment is important, more telling is the size of this investment relative to the management team's ability to invest. The commitment of the management team should also be backed by the support of the family, particularly the spouse, of each key team player. A positive family environment and spousal support allow team members to spend the 60 to 70 hours per week necessary to start and grow the company. One successful investor makes it a point to have dinner with the entrepreneur and spouse and even visit the entrepreneur's home before making an investment decision. According to one investor, "I find it difficult to believe an entrepreneur can successfully run and manage a business and put in the necessary time when the home environment is out of control."

The second criterion is that the product/market opportunity must be unique, having a differential advantage in a growing market. Securing a unique market niche is essential since the product or service must be able to compete and grow during the investment period. This uniqueness needs to be carefully spelled out in the marketing portion of the business plan, and is even better when it is protected by a patent or a trade secret.

The final criterion for investment is that the business opportunity must have *significant capital appreciation.* The exact amount of capital appreciation varies, depending on such factors as the size of the deal, the stage of development of the company, the upside potential, the downside risks, and the available exits. An equity investor typically expects a 40 to 60 percent return on investment in most investment situations.

BOOTSTRAP FINANCING

One alternative to acquiring outside capital that should be considered is bootstrap financing. This approach is particularly important at start-up and in the early years of the venture when capital from debt financing (i.e., in terms of higher interest rates) or from equity financing (i.e., in terms of loss of ownership) is more expensive.

In addition to the monetary costs, outside capital has other costs as well. First, it usually takes between 3 and 6 months to raise outside capital or to discover there is no outside capital available. During this time, the entrepreneur may not be paying enough attention to the important areas of his or her business such as marketing, sales, product development, and operating costs. When a business needs capital, it is usually when it can least afford the time to raise it. One company's CEO spent so much time raising capital that sales and marketing were neglected to such an extent that the forecasted sales and profit figures on the pro forma income statements were not met for the first 3 years after the capital infusion. This led to investor concern and irritation that, in turn, required more of the CEO's time.

Second, outside capital often decreases a firm's drive for sales and profits. One successful manager would never hire a person as one of his commission salespeople if he or she "looked too prosperous." He felt that if a person was not hungry, he or she would not push hard to sell. The same concept can apply to some externally funded companies that may have the tendency to substitute outside capital or government grants for income.

Third, the availability of capital increases the impulse to spend. It can cause a company to hire more staff before they are needed and to move into more costly facilities. A company can easily forget the basic axiom of venture creation: staying lean and mean. Examples of companies successfully growing by staying lean and mean and using internal capital instead of outside capital include Civco Medical Instruments and Metrographics Printing and Computer Services. Civco Medical Instruments, a manufacturer of medical accessories, was founded by Victor Wedel, formerly chief technologist at the University of Iowa, in 1982. The company started with $100 and had a bank loan as an early capital source. The company achieved sales of $3.2 million and $800,000 pretax profits and 35 employees. Similar results occurred for Metrographics, which was founded in 1987 by Andrew Duke, Jeff Bernstein, and Patrick Neltri with $100 from each entrepreneur. The company, which distributes printing and computer services, has grown to over $2.5 million in sales and 12 employees.

Fourth, outside capital can decrease the company's flexibility. This can hamper the direction, drive, and creativity of the entrepreneur. Unsophisticated investors are particularly a problem as they often object to a company moving away from the focus and direction outlined in the business plan that attracted their initial investment. This attitude can encumber a company to such an extent that the needed change cannot be implemented or else is implemented very slowly after a great deal of time and effort has been spent in consensus building. This can substantially demoralize the entrepreneur who likes the freedom of not working for someone else.

Finally, outside capital may cause disruption and problems in the venture. Capital is not provided without the expectation of a return, sometimes before the business should be giving one. Also, particularly if certain equity investors are involved, the entrepreneur is under pressure to continuously grow the company so that an initial public offering (IPO) can occur as soon as possible. This emphasis on short-term performance can be at the expense of the company's long-term success.

In spite of these potential problems, an entrepreneur at times needs some capital to finance growth, which would be too slow or nonexistent if only internal sources of funds were used. Outside capital should only be sought after all possible internal sources of funds have been explored. And when outside funds are needed and obtained, the entrepreneur should not forget to stay intimately involved with the basics of the business, form the right capital structure, and obtain the funds in the right form from the right source.

12

Managing the Cash

PROFILE—SHARON THOMAS-RAY

In 1995, as an assignment to develop a product and create an introduction plan for a marketing class at National Lewis University in Chicago, Sharon Thomas-Ray decided to address the problem she had observed while working at a fashion show—the length of time it took models to tie their neckties to the right length. To solve the problem, she developed an adjustable tie for men and women with a zipper known as the Y-Tie. After obtaining a patent on the Y-Tie in 1998, Sharon Thomas-Ray decided to actually introduce her new product into the market.

Following the usual approach of a small start-up company, she sold some ties to some small stores in the Chicago market. The Y-Tie retailed for $12.95 for the polyester version and $24.95 for the silk version. Progress was slow and the company was experiencing severe cash-flow problems. Some publicity on the *WGN Morning News* and in the *Chicago Sun Times* resulted in an $8000 order from the Salvation Army. This order prompted Sharon to tackle the lack of sales and cash-flow problem by pursuing big orders instead of trying to sell to smaller accounts. This idea led to entrance into the uniform market, which has a large nationwide network of uniform shops, through Kale Uniforms, a major uniform distributor in the Chicago area.

With the assistance of Kale, Sharon Thomas-Ray obtained the Chicago Transit Authority and Pace Bus Service as customers in 1999 and 2000. The company addressed the restaurant uniform market through Sharon attending the 2000 and 2001 National Restaurant Association Shows and selling through a Chicago-area restaurant distributor—Chef Direct. Given this success, the company was an exhibitor at the National Association of Uniform Manufacturers and Distributors, where 15 independent sales agents were obtained. Today the company sells its Y-Ties through its established distributors, independent sales agents, Fechheimer catalogues, and the company's website (www.ytie.com). Sales in 2002 were around $750,000.

Like Sharon Thomas-Ray, sometimes an entrepreneur should not take the conventional approach of starting a sales plan by selling to small local customers. Instead, they should not be intimidated and go after large buyers who are often easier to sell to and then deal with in terms of the cash flow than small customers with limited budgets. Entrepreneurial businesses at all stages have severe problems when incoming cash does not at least offset costs and other expenses. They are experiencing too high a burn rate—the amount of money the company loses (is burning through) each month. This may be the biggest mistake of entrepreneurs wanting to grow their business, or at least survive, as what really counts is cash. This process of managing your cash is the focus of this chapter so you can avoid one of the biggest mistakes—running out of cash.

BASIC CONCEPT OF THE CASH FLOW STATEMENT

The statement of cash flow, one of the most important statements for the entrepreneur, indicates where cash comes from and how it is spent. Since cash flows are cash receipts and cash payments, the statement of cash flow reflects the cash receipts and disbursements of the major activities of the entrepreneur's company—operating, investing, and financing. The statement explains the causes for any changes in the cash balance.

By doing this, the statement of cash flow has three primary purposes for the entrepreneurial company: evaluate the entrepreneur's decisions, predict future cash flows, and show the relationship of net income to changes in cash in the company. In terms of decisions, the statement of cash flow reports the company's investment in assets, such as plant and equipment, providing a basis for evaluating the decision-making capability of the entrepreneur and the management team. The second purpose of the statement of cash flow, predicting future cash flow, is critical for the entrepreneur to make sure the venture does not run out of cash. Cash, not reported accounting income, pays salaries, suppliers, and taxes. Usually, past cash receipts and disbursements are good predictors of future ones. Finally, the statement of cash flow shows the relationship of net income to changes in cash. Typically net income and cash move together—high levels of income should lead to increases in cash. When this is not the case, problems can occur and can become so severe that, even if the entrepreneur's company is earning net income, if there is insufficient cash the company can fail. Also, the cash-flow statement can determine the ability of the entrepreneur to pay interest and principal to creditors and, when appropriate, dividends to shareholders.

ACTIVITIES IN A CASH-FLOW STATEMENT

The three activities shown in the cash-flow statement, operating, investing, and financing, are indicated in Table 12-1. Since operating activities create revenues and expenses from the entrepreneur's company doing business, these affect the income statement of the company. While the income statement reports the accrual-basis effects, the statement of cash flow reports the impact of the operating activities on cash. The largest cash inflow from operations is collecting cash from customers resulting from the successful sales of the entrepreneur's products or services; another is the cash inflow from interest from such things as loans. The receipts from operating activities in the example in Table 12-1 were $252,000. The cash outflow of operating activities included payments to suppliers, employees, interest expense,

Table 12-1. Example statement of cash flows for the year ended December 31, 2002 (amounts in thousands of dollars).

Cash flows from operating activities:		
Receipts:		
Collections from Customers	244	
Interest Received on Notes Receivables	8	
Total Cash Receipts		252
Payments:		
To Suppliers	(120)	
To Employees	(53)	
For Interest	(14)	
For Income Tax	(10)	
Total Cash Payment		(197)
Net Cash Inflow from Operating Activities		55
Cash Flows from Investing Activities:		
Acquisition of Small Equipment	(10)	
Acquisition of Machinery	(150)	
Net Cash Outflow from Investing Activities		(160)
Cash Flows from Financing Activities:		
Proceeds from Issuance of Long-Term Debt	70	
Proceeds from Bank Loan	20	
Net Cash Inflow from Financing Activities		90
Net Decrease in Cash		(15)
Cash Balance December 31, 2001		20
Cash Balance December 31, 2002		5

and income taxes, which in this example amounted to $197,000, leaving a net cash inflow from operating activities of $55,000. Every entrepreneur should try to achieve a large positive operating cash flow as the operations of the company needs to be the main source of the company's cash for the company to be successful in the long run.

Investing activities will positively or negatively impact the cash position resulting from the operating activities. Purchase of equipment, machinery, a building, trucks, or supplies are all investing activities that have negative cash outflows. Investing activities are related to the long-term health of the business as they lay the foundation for the future operations of the company. In our example there are two investing activities—the acquisition of office equipment of $10,000 and the acquisition of machinery of $150,000, making the net cash outflow from investing activities $160,000.

The last type of activity on the statement of cash flow, financing activities, is related to the long-term liability accounts and/or the owner's equity account from the balance sheet of the company. Financing activities include obtaining cash from investors or creditors needed to start and grow the company. Financing activities can be positive ones such as issuing stock, borrowing money by issuing notes, obtaining a bank loan, or issuing bonds. They also can have a negative impact on cash when they are outflows such as paying dividends, buying back stock, or paying off long-term loans or bonds. The financing activities shown in Table 12-1 brought in $90,000—$70,000 from issuing long-term debt and $20,000 from a bank loan. Since the entrepreneur's company began the year with cash of $20,000, but total cash assets decreased by $15,000 in 2002, the year ended with a remaining positive cash balance of $5000.

A summary of the cash receipts and disbursements in the three major categories of business activities is indicated in Figure 12-1. Again, since cash is king, a positive cash flow (cash receipts greater than cash disbursements) from the company's operating activities is needed as soon as possible in the life of the company.

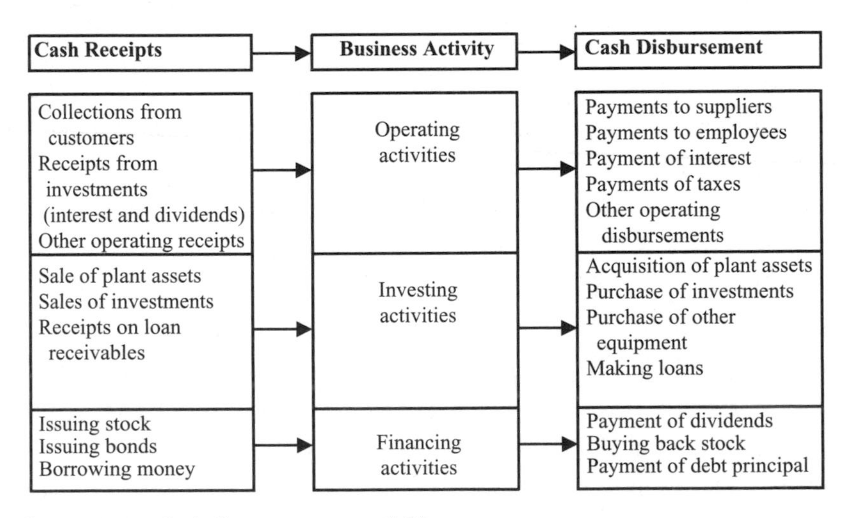

Figure 12-1. Cash-flow statement activities.

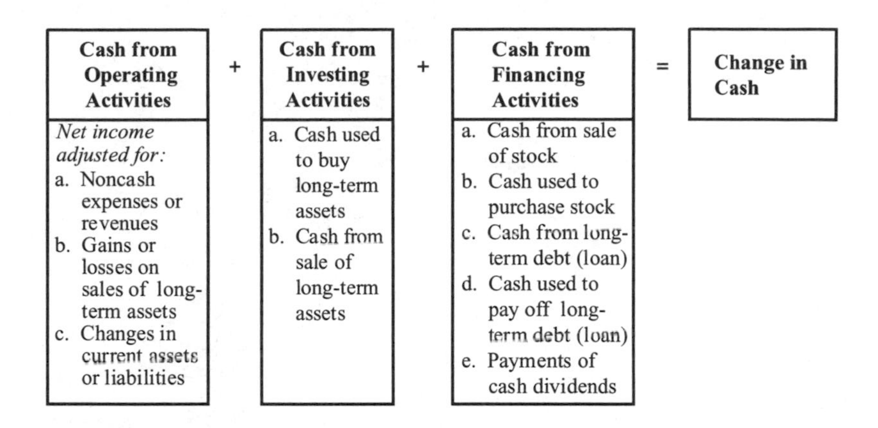

Figure 12-2. Cash-flow statement changes.

Another way for the entrepreneur to look at this important area of cash flow is indicated in Figure 12-2, where a format is used to explain the change in cash during a specified period of time.

THE CASH CYCLE

In order to maximize the cash flow and have as much cash as possible for the business, an entrepreneur needs to understand the cash cycle as indicated in Figure 12-3. The objective for the entrepreneur is to make the cycle spin more rapidly, therefore producing cost savings and cash. Specifically, the goal is to shorten the time between purchasing the raw materials and collecting cash from the customer, which requires that particular attention be paid to reducing production times, size and timing of all inventories, the time needed for collecting cash from the customer, and reducing the size of account receivables.

Let us see how cash can be freed up by looking at H&P Associates, a small entrepreneurial firm. The company had sales of $480,000; cost of sales (inventory sold) of $360,000; current inventory of $90,000; and accounts receivable of $60,000. The company has a current inventory turn of 4 times, which is 3 months, and an accounts receivable turn of 8 turns, which is 1.5 months. If the entrepreneur can increase the sales and improve the inventory turn to 6 turns, which

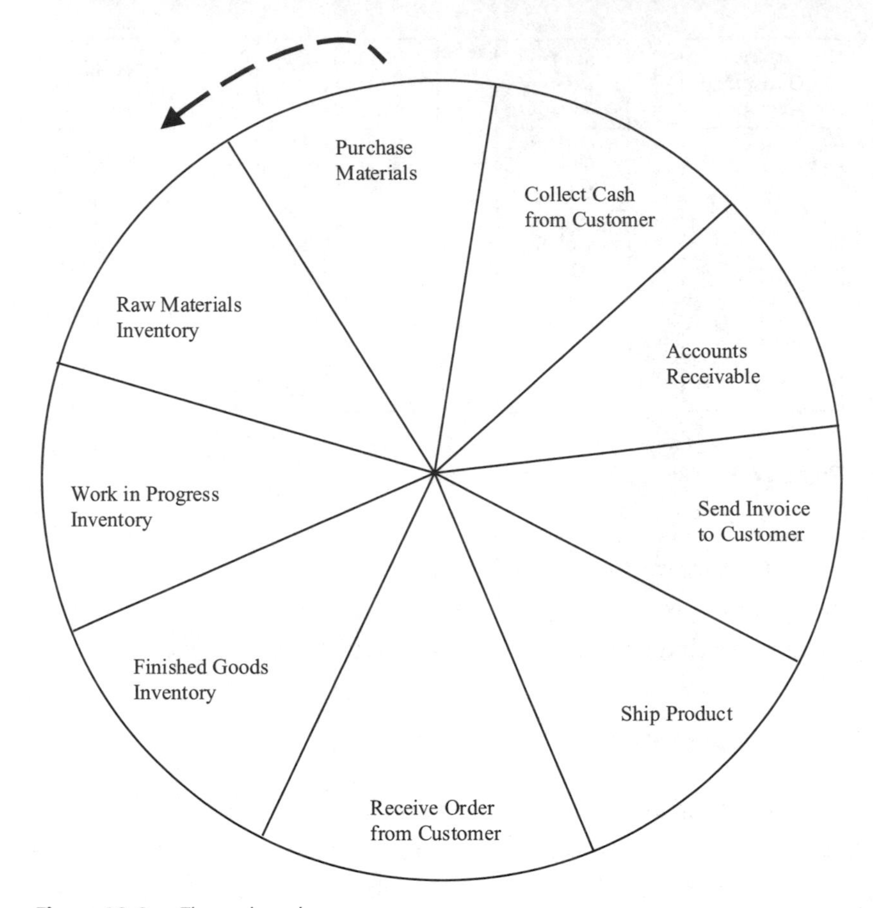

Figure 12-3. The cash cycle.

is 2 months, inventory costs would be reduced by $30,000. If accounts receivables were improved to 12 turns, or monthly, accounts receivable would be improved by $20,000. This would produce $50,000 ($30,000 + $20,000) in freed-up cash for the entrepreneurial company.

The key is to free up cash for your company in every way possible, particularly by minimizing the days in the cash cycle. There should be the minimum number of days in the raw materials inventory, work in process inventory, finished goods inventory, and accounts receivable, and the maximum number of days (as long as suppliers are satisfied) in accounts payable. Each of these can be calculated using the material shown in Table 12-2. The company's cash cycle begins once

Table 12-2. Days in the cash cycle.

Area	Calculation
Days in Raw Materials Inventory	$\frac{\text{Average Raw Materials Inventory}}{\text{Cost of Raw Materials}} \times 365 \text{ Days}$
Days in Work in Process Inventory	$\frac{\text{Average Work in Process Inventory}}{\text{Cost of Goods Sold}} \times 365 \text{ Days}$
Days in Finalized Goods Inventory	$\frac{\text{Average Finalized Goods Inventory}}{\text{Cost of Goods Sold}} \times 365 \text{ Days}$
Days in Accounts Receivable	$\frac{\text{Average Accounts Receivable}}{\text{Credit Sales}} \times 365 \text{ Days}$
Days in Accounts Payable	$\frac{\text{Average Accounts Payable}}{\text{Cost of Goods Sold} - \text{Labor}} \times 365 \text{ Days}$

the accounts payable are paid and lasts through raw materials inventory, work in process inventory, finished goods inventory, sale of the goods, invoicing the customer, and collecting the accounts receivable. The shorter this time period, the more cash the company has and the less probability of running out of cash and failing.

ACCOUNTS RECEIVABLE MANAGEMENT

One of the biggest areas of cash drain that needs to be carefully monitored by the entrepreneur is accounts receivable. There are three major factors influencing accounts receivable: cash discounts for early payment, credit terms offered, and the credit risk the entrepreneur's company is willing to assume. It may appear smart to collect your cash earlier than the typical 30, 60, or sometimes even 90 days of some channel members by offering terms such as a 2 percent discount if paid in 10 days of receipt of invoice and net 30 days. However, this only should be done with certain channel members. Some large retail chains will take the discount offered (in this case 2 percent of the amount of the invoice) and still pay the entrepreneurial company (less the discount) in their usual time, which is usually somewhere between 60 and 90 days depending on when the invoice is received within the company's standard payment cycle. Offering payment terms (which creates accounts receivable) means that one is assuming the credit risk that the purchaser will pay the debt in a timely manner.

Two basic principles should guide the entrepreneur in establishing an executive credit policy that drives accounts receivable. First, the longer the credit terms given to the purchaser, the lower the present value of the sale. Second, the greater the credit risk of the purchaser, the greater the loss in value of the sale.

INVENTORY MANAGEMENT

Containing the costs of inventory is another important way the entrepreneur can affect the cash cycle and therefore avoid the mistake of running out of cash. Inventory control is important to the entrepreneur as it is an expensive asset and requires careful balancing of just enough supply to meet demand for finished goods. If inventory is low and the firm cannot meet demand on time, sales can be lost. On the other hand, carrying excess inventory can be costly, either because of excessive handling and storage costs or because it becomes obsolete before being sold. Growing ventures typically tie up more cash in their inventory than in any other part of the business. Skolnik Industries, a $10 million manufacturer of steel containers for storage and disposal of hazardous materials, recently developed an inventory control system that allows them to ship products to their customers within 24 to 48 hours. This was accomplished with a very lean inventory due to the installation of a computerized inventory-control system that allows the firm to maintain records of on-hand supplies on a product-by-product basis. In addition to this capability, the system allows the company to monitor gross margin return on investment, inventory turnover, percentage of orders shipped on time, length of time to fill back orders, and percentage of customer complaints to shipped orders. Software to accomplish these goals is readily available and in many cases can even be modified to meet the exact needs of the business. The reports from this system are generated every 2 to 4 weeks in normal sales periods and weekly in heavy sales periods. This system not only provides Skolnik with an early warning system but also frees up cash normally invested in inventory and improves the overall profitability of the firm.

Regardless of the inventory costing method used, it is important for the entrepreneur to keep careful records of inventory. Perpetual inventory systems can be structured using computers or a manual system. As items are sold, inventory should be reduced. To check the inventory balance, it may be necessary to physically count inventory periodically.

13

Valuing a Business

PROFILE—JOHN OSHER

Following short careers in carpentry and owning and operating small retail stores selling earrings and older-style clothing, John Osher spent much of his life inventing things and selling them to big companies. One of his inventions was the Spin Pop, which was a team effort with John Nottingham and John Spirk, principals of a Cleveland industrial design firm and the company's patent lawyer, Lawrence Blaustein. Spin Pop was a lollipop attached to a battery-powered plastic handle that spun around when a button was depressed. Spin Pop was sold to the Hasbro Company in a multimillion-dollar deal.

After the sale, the group was looking for a new idea to develop. Part of that effort was walking through retail stores looking for possibilities for a product that would cost very little and that everyone could use. The idea for a $5 electric toothbrush came while in a Wal-Mart store when the group saw electric toothbrushes from such companies as Sonic and Interplak costing more than $50. Given its high price it was no wonder that electric toothbrushes accounted for such a small amount of total toothbrush sales. John Osher and the group wanted to design an electric toothbrush that sold for just $1 more than the most expensive manual brand using the Spin Pop technology. They wanted to create value in the product, and then exit by selling the product (the company) to Procter & Gamble. Why Procter & Gamble? The group saw that Crest was losing its dominant market position to Colgate, in part due to Colgate's launching its "Total" theme, emphasizing the whitening versus cavity-fighting attributes of Crest. P&G probably would be extremely interested in doing anything to regain its top position.

After spending 18 months in developing and then sourcing a high-quality brush in China, costing no more than $5 including batteries, John Osher and the group had to decide how to prove that the product could sell so that a good price could be obtained from P&G. Since the group could not afford to advertise and still retain the low $5 price, they designed a unique packaging method. The "Try Me" package allowed the consumer to turn the brush on in the store before purchasing it. Dr. John's Spin Brush was tested in a Midwest discount chain, Meijer Inc., in October 1999, and outsold the leading manual toothbrush 3 to 1. Using the sales data from Meijer's stores, Walgreen Co. was convinced to start carrying the product as well. Wal-Mart followed after a Phoenix Wal-Mart sold 240 Spin Brushes over one weekend.

Sales of Dr. John's Spin Brush reached 10 million in 2000, tripling the existing 3 million electric toothbrush market in the United States. The impressive sales made it easy for John Osher to have a meeting with P&G management in July 2001, particularly since Colgate had recently launched Act Brush, an electric toothbrush priced at $19.95. A team headed by Darin Yates was established to evaluate Spin Brush. In one test using a panel of 24 consumers, 23 raved about the Spin Brush product and wanted to take it home. All the positive feedback and sales caused a deal to be structured and closed in January 2002 just 6 months after the initial meeting. P&G agreed to pay $165 million up front—nearly 4 times the company's prior year sales of $43 million—and pay an earn-out over the next 3 years based on a formula tied to financial results. Also, John Osher and two others were hired by P&G for a 3-year period to keep the Spin Brush project entrepreneurial. Sales were exceptional, selling in about 35 countries by 2002. P&G and the four Spin Brush founders agreed in March 2002 to an early payout of $310 million, at which time John Osher's contract ended; this $310 million payment combined with the initial up-front payment of $165 million resulted in the Spin Brush sale of $475 million. What became of John Osher? He is presently developing another product idea while being the Entrepreneur in Residence at the Weatherhead School of Management of Case Western Reserve University.

As with John Osher, there are few challenges facing an entrepreneur that are as complex and difficult as the valuation of his or her own company or the valuation of a business to acquire. The valuation is complicated by the fact that the buyer and/or seller may be more interested in something else than the specific value. The seller, for example, may want to sell his or her business over time and be paid not only for the present value but for the increased value over time. The buyer, on the other hand, may only be interested in the value of the business today, not in any future value that may or may not occur. For an agreement to be reached, the valuation method for determining an agreeable purchase price must take into account both events that probably will occur and events that probably will not occur. While there are several methods for appraising a business, the value of a business to a buyer who plans on managing and growing it may be different from that to a buyer who is only interested in the business as an investment. Since the appraisal (valuation) of a business is based on the facts and circumstances surrounding the particular business, a technique employed in one valuation situation may not be right in another valuation.

This chapter explores this common entrepreneurial mistake by looking at possible processes for (1) establishing valuation methods, (2) valuing assets, (3) valuing liabilities, (4) calculating ratio analysis, and (5) determining the correct purchase price.

VALUATION METHODS

There are a wide variety of valuation methods that an entrepreneur can use to value his or her business or a business for possible acquisition or merger. An analysis of sales and profits and an evaluation of the business assets are the overall ways an entrepreneurial business is valued. The historic sales and profit analysis establishes a base for projecting the future profitability of the business. When the business being valued is an active, growing, ongoing concern, the profit-producing capacity becomes a key to its value.

Once the income-producing ability of a business or the business to be acquired is determined, its value is estimated by applying some multiple to this number or to its projected future profits. The multiplier used (as well as the method) will depend on the characteristics of the business, its track record, the time of operation, the nature of the industry, and overall future prospects. The higher the level of risk, generally the lower the multiplier.

To determine the past profit capability of a business, generally 5 years of historical data is obtained if available. This data should be compared with industry data and specifically to businesses of similar size and nature within the industry. The future profitability of the industry as well as the business should be used to adjust the valuation upward or downward. Adjustments to the past income statements and balance sheets of the entrepreneur's business or the business to be acquired may have to be made to permit a valid comparison with the financial information available for other similar businesses. This is particularly a problem for businesses that are privately held.

Some other factors need to be considered when determining an appropriate valuation. First, the relative position of the business being valued with respect to other comparable businesses needs to be taken into account. Second, whenever another similar type of business recently has been sold, its purchase price should be taken into account in the final valuation. Finally, the form by which the valuation is implemented, and its tax consequences to both buyer and seller, need to be factored into the final valuation.

There are several methods for appraising a business, as indicated in Table 13-1. Each one will result in a different valuation for the same business. The methods include the fixed price, book value, multiple of earning, price/earnings ratio, discounted cash flow, return on investment, replacement value, liquidation value, excess earnings, and market value. A description of each method is provided in Table 13-1.

Table 13-1. Methods for valuation of a venture.

Method	Description/Explanation
Fixed price	• Two or more owners set initial value • Based on what owners "think" business's is worth • Uses figures from any one or combination of methods • Common for buy/sell agreements
Book value (known as balance sheet method)	1. *Tangible book value:* Set by the business's balance sheet Reflects net worth of the firm Total assets less total liabilities (adjusted for intangible assets) 2. *Adjusted tangible book value*: Uses book value approach Reflects fair-market value for certain assets Upward/downward adjustments in plant and equipment, inventory, and bad debt reserves
Multiple of earnings	• Net income is capitalized using a price/earnings ratio (net income multiplied by P/E number) • 15% capitalization rate is often used (equivalent to a P/E multiple of 6.7, which is 1 divided by 0.15) • High-growth businesses use lower capitalization rate (e.g., 5%, which is a multiple of 20) • Stable businesses use higher capitalization rate (e.g., 10%, which is a multiple of 10) • Derived value is divided by number of outstanding shares to obtain per-share value
Price/earnings ratio (P/E)	• Similar to return on investment approach • Determined by price of common stock divided by after-tax earnings • Closely held firms must multiply net income by an appropriate multiple, usually derived from similar publicly traded corporations • Sensitive to market conditions (prices of stocks)
Discounted future earnings (discounted cash flow)	• Attempts to establish future earning power in current dollars • Projects future earnings (5 years), then calculates present value using a discounted rate • Based on "timing" of future income that is projected

Table 13-1. (*Continued*)

Method	Description/Explanation
Return on investment (ROI)	• Net profit divided by investment • Provides an earnings ratio • Need to calculate probabilities of future earnings • Combination of return ratio, present value tables, and weighted probabilities
Replacement value	• Based on value of each asset if it had to be *replaced* at current cost • Firm's worth calculated as if building from "scratch" • Inflation and annual depreciation of assets are considered in raising the value above the reported book value • Does *not* reflect earning power or intangible assets
Liquidation value	• Assumes business ceases operation • Sells assets and pays off liabilities • Net amount after payment of all liabilities is distributed to shareholders • Reflects "bottom value" of a firm • Indicates amount of money that could be borrowed on a secured basis • Tends to favor seller since all assets are valued as if converted to cash
Excess earnings	• Developed by the U.S. Treasury to determine a firm's intangible assets (for income tax purposes) • Intent is for use only when there is no better method available • Internal Revenue Service refers to this method as a last resort • Method does not include tangibles with estimated useful lives (i.e., patents, copyrights)
Market value	• Needs a "known" price paid for a similar business • Difficult to find recent comparisons • Methods of sales may differ—installment vs. cash • Should be used only as a reference point

Some approaches use comparable publicly held companies and the prices of these companies' securities. This search for a similar company is both an art and a science. First, the company must be classified in a certain industry, since companies in the same industry share similar markets, problems, economies, and potential or actual sales and earnings. The review of all publicly traded companies in this industry classification should evaluate size, amount of diversity, dividends, leverage, and growth potential until the most similar company is identified. The valuation results are not completely accurate unless a truly comparable company is found.

The book value approach uses the adjusted book value, or net tangible asset value, to determine the firm's worth. The major problem in this approach is that the book value of the assets is usually different from the fair market value of the assets and therefore needs to be adjusted. Adjusted book value is obtained by making the necessary adjustments to the stated book value by taking into account any depreciation (or appreciation) of plant and equipment and real estate, as well as necessary inventory adjustments that result from the accounting methods employed. The basic procedure shown in Table 13-2 can be used.

Since the book valuation approach involves simple calculations, its use is particularly good in the following: relatively new businesses, businesses where the sole owner has died or is disabled, and businesses with speculative or highly unstable earnings.

The earnings approach is the most widely used method of valuing a company, since it provides the potential investor with the best estimate of the probable return on investment. The potential earnings are calculated by weighting the most recent operating year's earnings after they have been adjusted for any extraordinary expenses that

Table 13-2. Book value approach.

Book value	$_______
Add (or subtract) any adjustments such as appreciation or depreciation to arrive at figure on next line—the fair-market value	$_______
Fair-market value (the sale of the company's assets)	$_______
Subtract all intangibles that cannot be sold, such as goodwill	$_______
Adjusted book value	$_______

Table 13-3. The factor approach.

Approach (in 000s)	Capitalized Value	Weight	Weighted Value
Earnings: $40 × 10	$400	0.4	$160
Dividends: $15 × 20	$300	0.4	$120
Book value: $600 × 0.4	$240	0.2	$ 48
Average: $328			
10% discount: $33			
Per-share value: $295			

would not have normally occurred in the operations of a publicly traded company. An appropriate price/earnings multiple is then selected based on norms of the industry and the investment risk. A higher multiple will be used for a high-risk business and a lower multiple for a low-risk business. For example, a low-risk business in an industry with a 7-times-earnings multiple would be valued at $4.2 million if the weighted average earnings over the past 3 years was $0.6 million (7 times $0.6 million).

An extension of this method is the factor approach, wherein the following three major factors are used to determine value: earnings, dividend-paying capacity, and book value. Appropriate weights for the particular company being valued are developed and multiplied by the capitalized value, resulting in an overall weighted valuation. An example of the factor approach is shown in Table 13-3.

One valuation approach that gives the lowest value of the business is liquidation value. Liquidation value is often difficult to obtain, particularly when cost and losses must be estimated for selling the inventory, terminating employees, collecting accounts receivable, selling assets, and other closing-down activities. Nevertheless, it is also good for an investor to obtain a downside risk value in appraising a company.

One approach an entrepreneur can use to determine how much of the company a venture capitalist will want for a given amount of investment is indicated below:

$$\text{Venture capitalist ownership (\%)} = \text{VC \$ investment} \times \frac{\text{VC investment multiple desired}}{\text{Company's projected profits in year 5} \times \text{price earning multiple of comparable company}}$$

Consider the following example:

A company needs $500,000 of venture capital money.
The company is anticipating profits of $650,000.
The venture capitalist wants an investment multiple of 5 times.
The price/earnings multiple of a similar company is 12.

According to the calculations following, the company would have to give up 32 percent ownership in order to obtain the needed funds.

$$\frac{\$500{,}000 \times 5}{\$650{,}000 \times 12} = 32\%$$

Besides general valuation methods, when evaluating a company it is important to put a value on some of the most important parts of the company—its assets.

RATIO ANALYSIS

Another way to see how a company is performing is to calculate various ratios and compare these on a year-to-year basis as well as against industry averages or other benchmarks. Ratio analysis indicates how the business is performing in comparison to others in the industry. The comparison figures are available in industry reports, trade journals, companies' annual reports, the *Value Line Investment Survey*, or *Standard & Poor's Industry Surveys*. Most often calculated are activity ratios, leverage ratios, liquidity ratios, and profitability ratios.

Activity Ratios

There are several activity ratios that indicate how the business is managing its assets. Accounts receivable turnover indicates how fast the company is turning its credit sales into cash and is calculated using the following formula.

$$\text{Accounts Receivable Turnover} = \frac{\text{Credit Sales}}{\text{Accounts Receivable}}$$

The accounts receivable turnover is then used to determine the company's average collection period.

$$\text{Average Collection Period} = \frac{\text{Days per Year}}{\text{Accounts Receivable Turnover}}$$

The next most frequently calculated activity ratio—the inventory turnover ratio—shows how effectively the company is moving its inventory so that none becomes obsolete.

$$\text{Inventory Turnover} = \frac{\text{Cost of Goods Sold}}{\text{Average Inventory}}$$

Leverage Ratios

Leverage ratios indicate the degree the company's assets are financed by debt and are therefore subject to the claims of creditors. The debt to equity ratio indicates what percentage of owner's equity is debt.

$$\text{Debt to Equity} = \frac{\text{Total Liabilities}}{\text{Equity}}$$

The debt to assets ratio shows the percentage of the company's assets owned by creditors.

$$\text{Debt to Assets} = \frac{\text{Total Liabilities}}{\text{Total Assets}}$$

Liquidity Ratios

To find out how much of a company's current assets are available to meet short-term creditors' claims, liquidity ratios are calculated. Current assets are cash and other assets that will be converted into cash in one operating cycle (the time from the buying or manufacturing of products, having them in inventory, selling them, and receiving cash from purchasers). Two ratios are used to determine the liquidity of a business—the current ratio and the acid test ratio.

$$\text{Current Ratio} = \frac{\text{Current Assets}}{\text{Current Liabilities}}$$

$$\text{Acid Test Ratio} = \frac{\text{Current Assets} - \text{Inventory}}{\text{Current Liabilities}}$$

While industry averages do vary, a current ratio of 2 or greater usually indicates that a company can satisfy its short-term debt without too much trouble. The acid test ratio takes this one step further by indicating how easily this short-term debt can be paid without even liquidating inventory. The acid test ratio is most important for any company having significant seasonal sales or rapidly changing product lines.

Profitability Ratios

Probably the most important ratios indicate how well the business is performing and how much of any investment in the business would likely be returned from the future earnings of the business or growth in the value of its assets. These profitability ratios particularly need to be compared on a year-by-year basis, with previous figures of the business as well as industry averages, which can be found in such places as *Dun and Bradstreet Industry Norms and Key Business Ratios.*

The gross profit margin ratio indicates how much gross profit (sales revenue less cost of goods sold) is generated by net sales (gross sales less returns):

$$\text{Gross Profit Margin} = \frac{\text{Gross Profit}}{\text{Net Sales}}$$

The ratio most often used in evaluating profitability is the return on investment (ROI) ratio. The ROI ratio indicates how much the business earns on each dollar of assets after it pays interest and taxes.

$$\text{Return on Investment (ROI)} = \frac{\text{Net Profit}}{\text{Total Assets}}$$

Another ratio indicating the quality and effectiveness of the management team is the return on equity ratio. This ratio indicates how productively the company's resources are being used by calculating how much of each dollar invested is generating net income.

$$\text{Return on Equity Ratio} = \frac{\text{Net Profit}}{\text{Total Assets} - \text{Total Liabilities}}$$

Performing ratio analysis in these four areas indicates how well the entrepreneur or a potential acquisition candidate has managed by showing the efficiency in obtaining the highest possible return with the fewest resources.

DETERMINING THE PRICE FOR AN ACQUISITION

Some of the key factors used in determining the price of a potential business are the following: earnings (past and future potential), assets, owner's equity, stock value, customer base, strength of distribution network, personnel, and image. When these factors are difficult to value, the entrepreneur may want to get outside help. The price paid should provide the opportunity for the purchaser to get a reasonable payback and good return on the investment.

There are three widely used valuation approaches—asset, cash flow, and earnings—that the entrepreneur can use to determine a fair price (or value) of an acquisition. When using the asset valuation method, the entrepreneur is valuing the underlying worth of the business based on its assets. The four methods that can be used to obtain asset valuation are: book value, adjusted book value, liquidation value, or replacement value. Although the easiest method for assessing the value of the firm is book value, the figure obtained should only be a starting point since it reflects the accounting practices of the company. A better refinement of this figure is the adjusted book value, where the stated book value is adjusted to reflect the actual market value. The third method of valuing the assets of a potential acquisition company is to determine the amount that could be realized if the assets of the company were sold or liquidated and the proceeds used to settle all liabilities. This liquidation value reflects the valuation at a specific point in time. If the company continues operations successfully, the calculated value is low compared to the contribution of the assets. If the company encounters difficulties, the actual liquidation would probably yield significantly less than the amount calculated. The final method for valuing assets is the determination of replacement value or the current cost of replacing the tangible assets of the business.

Another way of evaluating a firm—which is particularly relevant for an entrepreneur who is attempting to appraise a return on investment and on time—is to calculate the prospective cash flow from the business. The following three types of cash flow are important: positive cash flow, negative cash flow, and terminal value. Positive cash flow is cash received from the operation of the business minus costs, except depreciation. A negative cash flow (indicating the possible acquisition is losing money) can even be a benefit to the taxes of the business or individuals. The final cash flow value, the terminal value, is a source of cash resulting from an entrepreneur selling the business.

A final evaluation method is earnings valuation. This method capitalizes earnings of a company by multiplying the earnings by the appropriate factor (the price/earnings multiple). Two critical issues in this evaluation procedure are the earnings and the multiple. The question of earnings involves determining the appropriate earnings period as well as the type of earnings. The earnings period can encompass historical earnings, future earnings under the present management and ownership, or future earnings under new management and ownership. The type of earnings used during the selected period can be earnings before interest and taxes (EBIT), operating income, profit before tax, or profit after tax. The EBIT is used more frequently as it indicates the earning power and value of the basic business without the effects of financing.

After the time period and type of earnings have been established, the final step in earnings evaluation is to select the appropriate price/earnings multiple. If the primary return from the investment will be in the form of a stock sale at some future time, it is appropriate to select a price/earnings multiple of a publicly traded stock similar to the company being evaluated in terms of the product; the nature of the industry; and the anticipated earnings, growth, and likely state of the stock market. Although this can be difficult, usually a value or at least a range of values can be ascertained.

FORMULATING AND DOING THE DEAL

The structure of the purchase price must also be defined when determining final purchase price. This means developing and outlining all aspects of the sale and including them in the final purchasing arrangement. The following areas need to be considered: amount of cash and its timing, consulting contracts, covenants not to compete, employment contracts, transfer of assets, continuation of any existing benefit programs, continuation (or termination) of any existing deferred compensation programs, and long- or short-term lease agreements.

In writing the final purchase (or sale) agreement it is important to be well represented by counsel. A top-notch experienced attorney should prepare a draft of a purchase (sale) agreement that incorporates all the items formulated, as well as any additional items deemed prudent. A fixed price for this work should be obtained. Since the experience of the attorney and his or her law firm has resulted in the drafting of numerous agreements for previous clients, this provides for items in other agreements to be considered for inclusion in the present agreement. Although the attorney selected has significant experience, this does not mean infallibility. The document should be carefully reviewed not only by the parties involved in the sale but by third-party advisors as well. This tenacity will allow for the most thorough valuation possible and thus a successful sale.

Index

About the Author

Robert D. Hisrich is the A. Malachi Mixon III Professor of Entrepreneurial Studies at Case Western Reserve University's Weatherhead School of Management, where he has received recognition for his research and is Chair of the Entrepreneurship and Strategy Divisions. He holds an MBA and a doctorate from the University of Cincinnati.

Professor Hisrich's research pursuits are focused on entrepreneurship and venture creation: entrepreneurial ethics, intrapreneurship, women and minority entrepreneurs, venture financing, and global venture creation. He teaches courses and seminars in these areas, as well as in marketing management and product planning and development. His interest in global management and entrepreneurship resulted in two Fulbright Fellowships in Budapest, Hungary, honorary degrees from universities in Russia and Hungary and being a visiting faculty member in universities in Austria, Australia, Ireland, and Slovenia.

Professor Hisrich serves on the editorial boards of several prominent journals in entrepreneurial scholarship and is the author or coauthor of over 200 research articles appearing in such journals as *Journal of Marketing, Journal of Marketing Research, Journal of Business Venturing, Journal of Small Business Finance, Small Business Economics, Journal of Developmental Entrepreneurship*, and *Entrepreneurship Theory and Practice*. He has authored or coauthored 13 books, including *Marketing: A Practical Management Approach*, and the recently published sixth edition of *Entrepreneurship: Starting, Developing and Managing a New Enterprise* (translated into six languages).